brilliant

employability skills

'Packed full of practical, easy to understand tips to demystify the process of preparing yourself for your future career. An essential read for all students starting uni!'

Gemma Kenyon, Head of Careers,
City Careers Service,
City, University of London

'The most direct, to-the-point and easy to read book on what employers are looking for in the graduates they recruit and the skills you will need to develop in order to stand out. This is a must-read for all students.'

Gareth Lewis, Head of Careers,
Employability and Enterprise,
Coventry University London

Pearson

At Pearson, we have a simple mission: to help people make more of their lives through learning.

We combine innovative learning technology with trusted content and educational expertise to provide engaging and effective learning experiences that serve people wherever and whenever they are learning.

From classroom to boardroom, our curriculum materials, digital learning tools and testing programmes help to educate millions of people worldwide – more than any other private enterprise.

Every day our work helps learning flourish, and wherever learning flourishes, so do people.

To learn more, please visit us at **www.pearson.com/uk**

brilliant

employability
skills

second edition

How to stand out from the crowd in the graduate
job market

Frances Trought

 Pearson

Harlow, England • London • New York • Boston • San Francisco • Toronto • Sydney • Dubai • Singapore • Hong Kong
Tokyo • Seoul • Taipei • New Delhi • Cape Town • São Paulo • Mexico City • Madrid • Amsterdam • Munich • Paris • Milan

PEARSON EDUCATION LIMITED

Edinburgh Gate
Harlow CM20 2JE
United Kingdom
Tel: +44 (0)1279 623623
Web: www.pearson.com/uk

First published 2012 (print and electronic)
Second edition published in Great Britain 2017 (print and electronic)

ISBN: 978-1-292-15890-7 (print)
      978-1-292-15891-4 (PDF)
      978-1-292-15892-1 (ePub)

British Library Cataloguing-in-Publication Data
A catalogue record for the print edition is available from the British Library

Library of Congress Cataloging-in-Publication Data
Names: Trought, Frances, author.
Title: Brilliant employability skills : how to stand out from the crowd in
   the graduate job market / Frances Trought.
Description: Second Edition. | New York : Pearson Education, 2017. | Series:
   Brilliant series | Revised edition of the author's Brilliant employability
   skills, 2012. | Includes bibliographical references and index.
Identifiers: LCCN 2016054666 (print) | LCCN 2016055863 (ebook) | ISBN
   9781292158907 (pbk.) | ISBN 9781292158907 (PDF) | ISBN 9781292158921
   (ePub) | ISBN 9781292158921
Subjects: LCSH: College graduates—Employment. | Employability. | Job
   hunting. | Career development.
Classification: LCC HD6277 .T76 2017 (print) | LCC HD6277 (ebook) | DDC
   650.1—dc23
LC record available at https://lccn.loc.gov/2016054666

10 9 8 7 6 5 4 3 2 1
21 20 19 18 17

Print edition typeset in Plantin MT Pro 10/14 by SPi Global
Printed by Ashford Colour Press Ltd., Gosport

In memory of Robert Trought.

To my six chilli peppers: Symphonie Trought, Jorrell Trought, Melodie Trought, Trinity Rene, Sydney Rene and Michael Rene. To my family and friends: Carol René, Karen Kufuor, Afia Kufuor, Neil Parillon, Ade Bola, Clare Edet, Thomas Anderson, Lex Showunmi, Sophie Barrow, Jonathon Barrow, Shirley Barrow, Ralph Macbain, Anthony Oshodi, Charlotte Oshodi, Caleb Oshodi, Jacqui Ricketts and Makgoadi Makgoba.

Contents

Foreword

I wrote an introduction to the first edition of this excellent book back in 2011, and when I was asked to write the foreword for this new edition, the obvious question was: What has changed in five years?

Clearly, on the surface a lot has changed: we are out of the 2009–13 recession and into a growing and relatively buoyant economy, with many more graduate jobs. The service sector – from banking and finance to hotel and catering – is booming again, especially in London and the big cities. Technology is even more dominant in our lives – and in the workplace – than ever before as we all seem to be 'knowledge workers' now. And there are jobs being advertised which didn't even exist in 2011 (what exactly does an IT scrum-master do?). Graduate earnings are inching up. This is a comparatively good time to graduate.

But the economic cycle is just that: a cycle. Risk and uncertainty are always around the corner. Who knows what world the graduate of 2020 will be faced with? What will the economy look like? What new jobs and careers will be available? What jobs will be superseded by machines and robots?

So this book deals with the underlying and eternal verities about job seeking. The most important of these is employability. And underpinning that is the work ethic. Without it, all that follows is merely window-dressing. And, of course, the work ethic is not a synonym for workaholic: it means industrious and hard-working, reliable and conscientious

Jobs come and go, careers flourish or flounder, but a person's basic employability – the ability to be employable – is the rock upon which the next job or career can be built. What does a person need to allow them to succeed and prosper in the twenty-first century economy in general and jobs market in particular? What skills and attributes, taught and learned, acquired and innate, would need to be identified and displayed?

Top-level communication skills are a prerequisite: speech, writing and personal appearance (body language), as an individual and as part of a team. Poor formal speech and txt wrtg put you on the back foot, as does an inability to use the most modern communication systems (Snapchat and Instagram among others as I write this in 2016). And empathy and emotional intelligence are human traits which computers cannot simulate.

The ability to gather information, analyse it, synthesise it and then apply it is a vital skill. Finally, the ability to learn new skills (and teach others) through formal and informal continuous professional development is essential.

All of these skills and abilities can be learnt. None of them are beyond anybody's reach. It is as often about attitude as it is ability, and attitudes can be trained through practice and hard work.

You may have noticed that employability does not demand a formal qualification. True, one cannot be a lawyer or a physicist without either a qualification or a degree or both, but the lawyers and physicists who languish in un- or underemployment are probably not displaying the underpinning employability traits outlined above.

So the message is clear: a degree is often necessary, but rarely sufficient. Jobs are for today, careers for the immediate future, but employability is for ever. And employability can be learnt, honed and practised. Oh, and it is never finished.

Mike Hill, CEO, Higher Education
Careers Services Unit and Graduate Prospects

About the author

Frances Trought is Head of Student Talent Development at Pearson Business School. She has a career in higher education that spans 14 years and has observed that increasingly the degree is just one piece of the puzzle to success upon graduation. Employability is a key issue that affects the success of all students. The graduate market is becoming more and more competitive, and students need to understand the employability skills valued by graduate recruiters. Employers are unable to differentiate students based purely on their academics, with 72% scoring a first or 2:1. As a result, extracurricular activities and work experience have risen in importance. Frances is a keen advocate of volunteering and continually promotes opportunities to students, as it is a great opportunity to gain skills and contribute to society. To this end, she has developed the Contribute Volunteering Award at Pearson Business School. Frances is passionate that students step out of their comfort zone at university to develop skills transferable to the work place. As a result, she develops workshops, delivers talks, provides one-to-one coaching and partners with organisations to bridge the gap between business and university.

If you would like to collaborate with Frances connect via LinkedIn: Frances Trought.

Author's acknowledgements

A big thank you to Steve Temblett, Eloise Cooke and Lisa Robinson for embarking on this journey with me.

Thank you to all the graduates who supplied their experiences to give practical advice to current students.

Thank you to all the organisations and individuals below who have provided valuable advice and examples:

- Helen Alkin, Head of Future Talent Recruitment, Marks and Spencer plc
- Hermon Amanuel, Business and Enterprise
- Damilola Anderson, President of Leicester African and Caribbean Society
- Gary Argent, Graduation Transitions
- Femi Awoyemi, Neet Engagement Coordinator, Elevation Networks
- Jamie Bettles, Managing Director, Intern China Ltd
- Martin Birchall, High Fliers Research Ltd
- Jo Blissett, Career Development Consultant, Career Quest
- Femi Bola, Director of Employability, University of East London
- Jon Brookstein, Head of Sport Development, British Universities & Colleges Sport
- Deborah Cardwell, Managing Director, UBC Worldwide

- Lucy Crittenden, Graduate Recruitment Manager, Reed Smith
- Jonathon Deakin, Client Director, PathMotion
- Julien Deslangles-Blanch, Regional Director, General Assembly London
- Megan Dunn, President, National Union of Students
- Rupert Emson, Managing Director, Vero Screening Ltd
- Alex Field, Marketing Manager, RMP Enterprise
- Sarah Flynn, Chair, ASET
- Patsy Francis, Director, Community Affairs, UBS
- John Garnett, Board Advisor, Consultant and former Managing Director
- Joshua Gouge, University Football Activator (volunteer) and Paramedic
- Amirah Hajat, Marketing Executive, RMP Enterprise
- Charles Hardy, Higher Education Leader, LinkedIn
- Mike Hill, CEO, Higher Education Careers Services Unit and Graduate Prospects
- Will Holt, Dean/Director of Pearson Business School, Pearson College London
- Joey Hosier, Customer Experience Manager, Marks and Spencer plc
- Ben Hughes, Vice Principal (academic delivery), Pearson Business School
- Stephen Isherwood, Chief Executive, Association of Graduate Recruiters
- Vincent Karremans, Founder and Managing Director, Magnet.me
- Karen St Jean-Kufuor, Principal Lecturer, Westminster Business School
- Andy Lancaster, Head of Learning and Development, CIPD

- Stefan Lloyd, Personal Trainer, SLR Fitness
- Johnny Luk, CEO, National Association of College and University Entrepreneurs
- Claire Miles, Managing Director, UK Customer Operations, British Gas
- Emma O'Connor, Senior Marketing and Communications Manager, MyKindaFuture
- Jack Preston, Owner, Yaantu
- Philip Preston, Network Manager, Chartered Institute of Marketing
- Denise Rabor, Founder, WOW Beauty and Leadership3sixty
- Carol René, Enterprise Lead Information and Data Architect, Shell International Petroleum Company
- Michael Rene, Undergraduate in Business Management with Economics
- Levi Roots, Entrepreneur, Levi Roots
- SHL People Performance
- Lex A Showunmi, Company Director and Conflict Management Trainer and Practitioner, 3S Partnerships Ltd
- Krystle Siaw, HR Manager, Premier Foods
- Sammie Stapleton, Head of UK Talent Channels, PwC
- Matt Stevens, Pearson Talentlens
- James Thomas and Apoorva Chaudry, Managing Directors, Pave
- Dr Yvonne Thompson CBE, Author, Marketing Guru and International Public Speaker
- Melodie Trought, Undergraduate at University of Sussex
- Michele Trusolino, COO, Debut
- Jamie Ward-Smith, CEO, Do-it.org
- Peter Westgarth, Chief Executive, The Duke of Edinburgh's Award

Publisher's acknowledgements

We are grateful to the following for permission to reproduce copyright material:

Graph on p.36 from UNESCO Institute for Statistics (UIS), http://www.uis.org, extracted July 2016; charts on pp. 91, 92, 94, 95–6, 118 and 139 from The Graduate Market 2016, © High Fliers Research Limited 2016.

Introduction

Every year 400,000 students in the UK graduate with a degree: what makes you stand out?

Whether you are studying for an English, history, business or engineering degree, the one thing you will all have in common is the fact that you all need to know how to market yourself. If your goal is to secure employment at the end of your degree or to start your own business, you will need to be able to convince a potential employer or investor that you are the perfect candidate. This is essential whether you wish to work in the private, public, third sector or become self-employed. Regardless of your field, there will always be competition and the need to stand out.

Marketing and graduate development

Marketing is often seen as a business-related activity, but it is essential for every successful graduate. While at university you are developing your own individual brand. When employability is viewed in its crudest form, we are all products attempting to sell our skills in the graduate marketplace. Consider the definition of a product as:

Anything that can be offered to a market for attention, acquisition, use or consumption that might satisfy a want or need.

(Kotler et al., 2016)

If we place this in the context of employability, the market would be the graduate employment market and the skills we seek to develop throughout our degree would represent 'anything that can be offered to a market', and we would hope that these skills would 'satisfy a want or need' of a potential employer.

As a result, strong analogies can be drawn between the development of a product and the development of graduates. The skills developed throughout a degree can be seen as the product features, the elements by which you seek to differentiate yourself from the competition – the other graduates in the marketplace.

If this analogy is extended and the marketing mix is considered, further correlations can be seen. The marketing mix is 'the set of tactical marketing tools – product, price, place and promotion – that the firm blends to produce the response it wants in the target market'. (Kotler et al., 2016, p. 78) The four 'P's (product, price, promotion and place) are used by firms and graduates to bring about their desired outcomes – recruiting the best graduates and gaining employment respectively. If we review all of these elements in this context, strong correlations can be drawn.

By definition, price relates to 'the amount of money charged for a product or service or the sum of the values that customers exchange for the benefits of having or using a product or service'. (Kotler et al., 2016, p. 324)

Salary is representative of price as it relates to the amount an employer is willing to pay for graduate services. As with price, salary is influenced by supply and demand and correlations can be drawn between surpluses and shortages in the marketplace dependent upon disciplines and skills. Competition also affects price and graduate recruiters will vary their price in order to make their offer attractive.

Salary, just like price, is influenced by the value a customer, in this case a graduate recruiter, attributes to acquiring new graduates. How important do companies see the acquisition of graduates to the development of their business and how much can they afford to pay?

Promotion in essence relates to how the value/benefit of a product is communicated to the target audience – in this instance, the way a graduate promotes his or her skills by the use of curriculum vitae, application forms, interviews and online profiles. Do not forget that graduate recruiters also want to recruit the best and so, in turn, adopt a promotion strategy in order to make their offer attractive to graduates by attending graduate recruitment fairs, advertising their graduate schemes and inviting students to career open days.

Place, as with product, relates to the distribution and the availability of the product. When looking for employment you will determine how far you are willing to travel and the location within which you are prepared to work. Graduate recruiters also distribute graduates throughout their organisation both locally and globally, representing a wide distribution network.

The career life cycle

The product life cycle (PLC) charts the progress of a 'product's sales and profits over its lifetime'. (Kotler et al., 2016) This model can also be modified to chart the development of a career. In the figure below, the PLC has been modified to represent the various stages of your career. At each stage, just as with a product, a strategy needs to be devised in order to sustain a positive result through continued career development represented by promotion, increase in salary or responsibility.

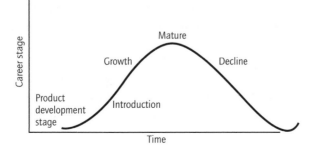

The product development stage represents the time you attend university and develop your skills prior to launching your product into the graduate market. The growth period represents the continued development of your career. It is at the mature stage that you have to make important career decisions in order to keep your career moving upwards.

Often companies in the mature phase will release an updated product with additional features to boost sales. At this stage the market has developed either due to the introduction of new technology or new processes and you have to update your skills or risk your skill set becoming outdated. To update skills students will often re-enter higher education at this stage to study for additional qualifications, either a Masters degree or professional qualifications. Others may return to education as a mature student to gain their first degree in order to enhance their career development.

The decline phase represents a shift in the market and highlights the fact that your skill set is not aligned with the job market. In many cases, this will result in redundancy. This can often kick-start the career life cycle, forcing a return to the product development stage.

? brilliant question

What stage are you at in your career life cycle? Are you still developing your product or returning to education to enhance your product? Or following redundancy, seeking to kick-start your career in a new direction?

Due to the increasingly competitive graduate market, and the increasing number of graduates in the marketplace, it has become imperative that graduates engage with the marketing of their skills in order to succeed. Employers can no longer differentiate between candidates based solely on their degree. You now have to consider what else you have to offer a potential employer.

As stated by McNair (2003), graduate employability has increased in importance 'because of the changing nature of the graduate labour market, mass participation in HE, pressures on student finance, competition to recruit students and expectations of students, employers, parents and government (expressed in quality audits and league tables)'.

What do we mean when we talk about employability?

brilliant definition

Employability

'a set of achievements – skills, understanding and personal attributes – that makes graduates more likely to gain employment and be successful in their chosen occupations, which benefits themselves, the workforce, the community and the economy'

(Mantze Yorke, 2006)

'a set of attributes, skills and knowledge that all labour market participants should possess to ensure they have the capability of being effective in the workplace – to the benefit of themselves, their employer and the wider community'

(CBI, 2011)

The CBI builds on this definition and identifies a set of employability skills, including:

- self-management
- communication and literacy
- team-working

- application of numeracy
- business and customer awareness
- application of information
- technology (IT)
- problem-solving
- positive attitude
- entrepreneurship/enterprise.

Source: Adapted from CBI, 2009

These skills are repeatedly identified as the core skills and attributes graduates need to be able to demonstrate upon graduation. The Global Graduates into Global Leaders Report (Diamond et al., 2008) stipulates that before graduates can even begin to consider developing the skills needed to compete on a global scale they need to ensure that they have developed the core skills and attributes listed above.

These skills are a prerequisite and are reinforced by the CMI report '21st Century Leaders' (2014), when employers were asked to identify the skills required from graduates. Communication (67%), problem-solving (48%) and team-building (47%) were listed as the top three skills valued by employers. As a result, the skills identified in the CMI report are still very relevant for graduates entering the market in 2017.

The I Brand employability model

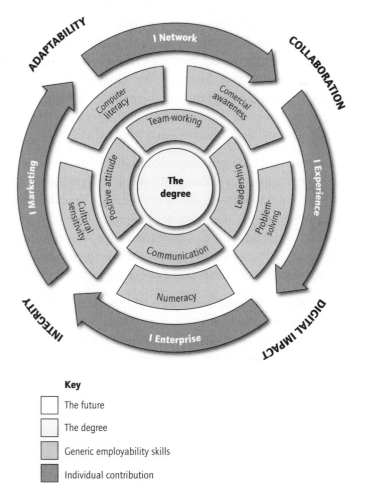

Key

☐ The future

☐ The degree

☐ Generic employability skills

☐ Individual contribution

The I Brand employability model incorporates these skills but recognises the importance of an individual's network, experience, enterprise and marketing skills. The model has been further developed to recognise the continually transforming and changing landscape within which organisations operate. It is important for graduates to not only develop their employability skills, but to also review how they can sustain their place within the marketplace.

A further four additional skills and attributes have been added to the I Brand employability model: integrity, adaptability, collaboration and digital impact. These four skills and attributes provide the students with the skills needed to future-proof their career development. The currency of experience is priceless when looking for a position. Repeatedly, employers will ask: 'Do you have any experience?' Often you can find yourself caught in a cycle whereby you can't get a job because you don't have any experience, but you can't get any experience because you don't have a job.

The elements of the I Brand employability model are discussed in further detail in Chapter 5. Essentially you are building your own individual brand to increase your employability – a brand being defined as 'a name . . . that identifies the products or services of one seller . . . and differentiates them from those of competitors'. (Kotler et al., 2016, p. 691) Your brand will help you stand out from the competition – other graduates in the graduate market.

Developing your I Brand encourages you to develop your own skills and differentiate your product, to communicate your brilliance to potential employers. From day one at university you need to think about how you will complete your course, but also how you will become a successful graduate. The difference is that being a successful graduate is not merely limited to gaining your degree but also includes developing additional skills that make you more marketable and as a result increase your employability.

The definitions of employability reference the development of skills and attributes that cannot be developed overnight. To attain these skills graduates cannot leave it to chance or leave it to the day before graduation. Students often believe that graduation is far away, but the three or four years will pass very quickly. Students need to actively engage with their career development to ensure that upon graduation they have developed a brand employers want to buy.

brilliant question

If your name was a brand, what would it stand for? What is your unique selling point (USP)? Reliability? Honesty? Trustworthiness?

The graduate market

Every year approximately 400,000 (HESA, 2015) UK graduates enter the job market, creating a situation where the demand for jobs far outstrips the supply. The market has surpassed pre-recession levels and *The Times'* top 100 graduate employers aim to increase their level of recruitment in 2016 by 7.5%.

Graduate recruiters have increased their expectations of graduate hires and are continually raising the stakes. In the summer of 2015, 77% of graduate employers required a 2:1 degree or above (AGR, 2016). The graduate recruitment market is competitive, but your time at university can be used to develop your skills to ensure you stand out.

How to use this book

This book is aimed at students studying at levels 4 and 5 of the National Qualifications Framework (first- and second-year university students) to encourage them to get involved in university and all that it offers. The exercises and information are still applicable to final-year and Masters students.

The book provides a range of exercises focused on self-exploration and self-development, in order to increase students' marketing potential. Students are encouraged to evaluate their current skills and devise an action plan to develop additional skills while at university through extracurricular activity.

Chapters 2, 3, 4 and 5 provide an overview of the job market and how to navigate your way through it. Students are presented with a number of options to gain work experience while at university and also research alternative avenues to enter their first-choice career. Chapter 6 focuses on how you can market your skills to potential employers and highlights the dos and don'ts of applying for jobs. Chapter 7 encourages students to recognise that this is not a one-off process but, to have a truly brilliant future, students need to continually review their skill sets to ensure they remain employable.

CHAPTER 1

Employability skills valued by employers

The man (woman) who has no imagination has no wings

Mohammed Ali

When completing an application form or attending an interview, employers need evidence of your abilities: your competences. It is essential that on the application form you are able to demonstrate your skills through your experiences, and the more varied the situation the better. Judge for yourself: Is hearing about a group exercise where students fundraised and trekked to Kilimanjaro more interesting to read about than a group exercise where students completed a presentation?

Students need to consider how they build their skills and where. University presents the opportunity not only to develop your skills but to challenge yourself and develop a wide set of experiences which set you apart from other graduates. Those students who fail to engage with extracurricular activities run the risk of not only limiting their development but also the range of examples they can use when completing an application form.

The development of soft skills has become increasingly important in today's economy. It is argued that soft skills contribute £88 billion to the UK economy and it is forecast to rise to £109 billion. The importance of soft skills is reflected by employers: 97% of employers believe that soft skills (in particular teamwork and communication) are essential to business success and are becoming increasingly more important than academic results. (Development of Economics Ltd, 2015)

This chapter will help you not only identify the skills valued by employers, but will also provide examples of how you can build these skills.

Self-management

Are you good with meeting deadlines? Are you organised? Do you use your own initiative?

If you can answer yes to these questions that's great, but if you can't manage yourself how can employers expect you to manage at work? Employers will expect you to be organised, punctual, working to deadlines and a self-starter. How you manage yourself and your approach to your work is key to being employable. Your first management role is self-management.

So what do we mean when we talk about self-management?

The CBI (2011) defines self-management as the 'readiness to accept responsibility, flexibility, resilience, self-starting, appropriate assertiveness, time management, readiness to improve own performance based on feedback/reflective learning'.

So how can you demonstrate you are good at self-management to an employer? The best way to demonstrate self-management is to look for examples in your current roles.

Do you work part time? Do you have responsibilities at home? Are you a mentor? These are excellent examples to demonstrate your ability to be responsible.

Employers will expect you to manage your time effectively and use your own initiative. Think of examples of where you have had to balance several assignment deadlines. How did you achieve this? Preparation, planning and organisation are essential for effective time management.

You can always learn from your experiences, so it is important to use feedback and reflection to see how you could have performed a task better. There is always room for improvement.

brilliant tip

Ask around and use feedback

You can gain valuable personal insight by gathering feedback from other students, your tutors or professors, mentors, friends and even family members. Ask them to think about both your strengths and areas you could improve on. For example:

● What should you do more of/keep doing?
● What should you do less of/stop doing?

Often others see you differently to how you see yourself and their answers will help you identify and build on your skills and areas of possible weaknesses.

Jo Blissett, Career Development Consultant, Career Quest

brilliant example

Worried about juggling a new volunteer role alongside your existing study commitments?

First, do not fret, as flexible volunteering where you offer your services as a volunteer as and when it suits you is now increasingly common. Second, your commitment to a volunteer role demonstrates not only motivation and drive to a potential employer, but organisational skills including planning and time management.

Meeting and dealing with new people through voluntary work will not only develop your patience and empathy towards others, but will demonstrate your ability to negotiate new and sometimes stressful scenarios. Being able to remain calm under pressure and think positively will help you to stand out both during the recruitment process and in the workplace. To get ▶

involved with a cause you're passionate about that has you jumping out
of bed on a rainy Sunday morning, take a look at Do-it.org (https://do-it.
org/), a national volunteering database.

Jamie Ward-Smith, CEO, Do-it.org

Self-management is an excellent indicator for an employer of
how you will cope in the workplace. You will have many tasks
to manage and demonstrating that you can multi-task successfully is a great skill. The ability to balance a commitment
alongside your academic studies is an excellent demonstration
of your time management, organisational and self-management
skills.

Teamworking

What do Barcelona FC, the United Nations and Great Ormond
Street Hospital have in common? They all achieve success through
teamwork. Each member of the team plays a vital role, and that
ensures their success.

The CBI (2011) stated that at the heart of teamworking is
'respecting others, cooperating, negotiating/persuading, con-
tributing to discussions, an awareness of interdependence with
others'.

In today's workforce this has become even more prevalent, and
as a result employers include teamworking exercises in their
selection processes to assess how well new graduates work in
teams. An assessment centre will often include a group exercise,
centred around a team of potential candidates working together
to find a solution to a problem. This provides the recruiters
with a good indication of how candidates work with others, as
often within the work environment, teams are formed across the
organisation.

Why is teamworking important?

So why is teamworking important? In today's rapidly changing marketplace organisations are faced with challenges, which cannot be addressed by one department. The challenge affects the organisation as a whole, and so teams are drawn from both across functions, but also globally. When devising solutions an organisation will need to have the knowledge from within its organisation and possibly from an expert consultant drawn from within its particular sector.

Collaboration is key in developing competitive advantage within the marketplace. This can involve collaborating externally with suppliers to develop new processes or new products. Working in teams enables an organisation to harness the expertise which exists both internally and externally. A team is much better placed to respond to the challenges faced in the competitive marketplace, as it enables the organisation to consider the challenge from many perspectives at once, and develop a solution that incorporates the needs of all of the business.

Teams come in different shapes and sizes. One size does not fit all. Throughout your time at university students will experience many different types of teams. As a member of a student society or club, students may find themselves working as a team to organise events, recruit members and fundraise. Other opportunities to work within a team are through sports, volunteering or even a group assignment.

Developing teamworking skills

University is the perfect place to develop teamworking skills. Often students work part time, which presents the opportunity to develop teamworking skills in a live environment, and the experience will enhance many other employability skills such as communication.

Whether you work in retail, fast food or tourism you will be part of a team and begin to understand the dynamics of working collectively towards a common goal. This goal could be to meet sales targets, to fundraise a specific amount or to collectively work together to enhance the customer experience.

Within the work environment teams exist in varying formats. Project teams will be created to address a specific business challenge. Often a team can be created virtually in order to capture the knowledge and experience of co-workers located nationally or even globally. Technology, in particular Skype and Google Hangouts, facilitate the ability to speak with teams virtually.

When working virtually and internationally communication skills become even more important, especially if the team is drawn globally. Time zones, cultures and customs become important factors to ensure the team works effectively and respectfully together.

▶ brilliant example

Virtual teams

Virtual teams are now commonplace and I have run them for many years. In a global business coupled with cost pressures, virtual team-working is now a business necessity and doing this right can add a huge competitive advantage. Here are my top five tips for managing a successful team.

- **Manage cultural dynamics:** Many virtual teams will incorporate different cultures and there is a need to manage conscious and unconscious biases to ensure the right behaviours and expectations.
- **Communication:** Always have a clear agenda and appropriate lead time for pre-reading meeting documents. Allocate who will manage minutes, actions and general communications.

- **Time zones:** There is a need to be sensitive regarding time zones, if possible. Try to rotate times so that alternate time slots can be scheduled to limit individuals being subjected to regular early mornings or late night calls.

- **Respect:** Set out clear rules to ensure all team members can be heard and the team actually listens. The chair has to carefully manage engagement.

- **Technology platform:** The communication platform has to be stable and accessible. It can be very disruptive to have platforms that are unreliable. This will hamper the progress but also the overall morale in the team.

Virtual teams are invaluable in the workplace, but it must be set up for success. The above dynamics are just a handful of critical success factors to manage a virtual team.

Carol René, Enterprise Lead Information and
Data Architect, Shell International Petroleum Company

What role would you play in a team?

Teams are created to provide a collective response to challenges faced by the organisation. What role do you think you would play in a team? Review these team roles and see which role reflects your skills.

- The project manager manages the team and takes on the responsibility of ensuring the project is delivered on time.

- The expert, as the name suggests, is a specialist in their field and highlights the impact of any solutions to the organisation and end-users.

- The innovator challenges the status quo and adopts a creative approach to tasks.

- The analyst evaluates all of the proposed solutions and highlights possible risks.

● The finisher ensures that all of the documentation and other outputs from the team tasks are submitted.

To review your role within ask your careers service to conduct a Myers Briggs test, which will highlight your position of strength in a team.

Certain skills and attributes are needed for a team to perform effectively. Respect is essential as you will not always be working with people you know or even like. Teams are often required to present their results or write a progress report, which will require good communication skills. The ability to negotiate or persuade is central to sourcing resources or convincing the team of a particular course of action. The success of the team is dependent on members sharing their knowledge and skills. A 'critical friend' asking challenging questions ensures that solutions are debated in full.

---

brilliant example

Conflict management and problem-solving

First, let me start by saying that when working in a team I believe conflict is inevitable and therefore unavoidable – even for those who really try their hardest to avoid it. Preparing yourselves in advance for any potential clashes by practising conflict management skills is a must if you wish to succeed in your chosen career.

One of the best ways to help you develop a constructive approach to conflict really begins long before you are even involved in one – by 'accepting' that conflict is inevitable and will occur at some point, as it will help you to positively prepare yourself. The ability to manage conflict in a constructive and positive manner is increasingly becoming a sought after 'soft skill' in the work environment.

How you manage the conflicts you face at work will play a huge part in your successes in life, as when carried out effectively, you will be able to create harmonious and respectful relationships which enhance the working environment around you. You will therefore increase your employability skills and begin to progress at work.

The top five qualities needed when managing conflict are the following:

- patience
- respect (for others)
- empathy
- (active) listening
- think win–win.

> Lex A Showunmi, Company Director and
> Conflict Management Trainer/Practitioner,
> 3S Partnerships Ltd

Teamworking is a vital part of any organisation. The structure and size of the team is dependent upon the nature of the task. Each member of the team plays a different role, which is equally important and contributes to the success of the project. In order for teams to work effectively team members must have a range of skills.

Business and customer awareness

Business and customer awareness is important to an employer as your opinions demonstrate how you can add value to their organisation. Employers will expect you to understand their markets, their customers and the challenges they face.

As stated by the CBI (2011) 'graduates should have a basic understanding of the key drivers for business success – including the importance of innovation and taking calculated risks – and the need to provide customer satisfaction and build customer loyalty'.

How do you develop specific sector knowledge?

An insight to your chosen industry sector can be gained by reading newspapers, journals and newsletters from professional bodies. This will not only help you with your employability skills, but you will find you have a better understanding of your lectures and assignments. Your industry knowledge will be more apparent in the conversations you have about your sector and the responses you give in interviews. Below are a few examples of how to stay abreast of your industry:

- Create a Google Alert to refer to a page.
- Company websites provide an insight into the industry and the challenges they face in the competitive market.
- Industry-specific events can help you meet people who work in the industry and give you an insight into the structure of the organisation and the various roles which exist.

Ultimately the best way to gain an insight into an industry is to gain work experience. Work shadowing, internships and placements all provide opportunities for you to not only understand the industry but to see if you want to work in it. As a result, you will gain an insight into how companies manage the users' experience and build brand loyalty. You can develop this knowledge by reflecting on your own experiences with companies. Customer retention is important for businesses as without customers there is no business. Review company websites and how they build loyalty with their customers.

Problem-solving

The CBI defines problem-solving as 'analysing facts and situations and applying creative thinking to develop appropriate solutions'.

Organisations continually face challenges from advancing technology, competitors and changing markets so they need employees who can develop innovative solutions that will keep them ahead of the competition. Graduates who are creative, innovative and use their own initiative are essential to developing solutions to the challenges of the future.

How do you develop problem-solving skills?

You already have problem-solving skills. You are faced with challenges every day in both your academic course and your personal life. The skills you use to address these problems are transferable to the workplace. Essentially all problem-solving revolves around 'gap analysis', the difference between a desired outcome and the actual outcome. Regardless of whether it is an academic problem or organising an event such as your brother's wedding you will need to follow a number of steps. These are defined by Bransford and Stein (1984) in their IDEAL problem-solving model, which can be used within a range of contexts.

Identify the problem. What are the essential elements of the problem?

Define the problem through thinking about it and sorting relevant information.

Explore solutions. What are the advantages and disadvantages of each solution?

Act on strategies.

Look back and evaluate the effects of your activity.

Finding a solution may need you to develop additional employability skills. For example, you may need to create a diverse team, use your communication and IT skills to present your ideas or use your numeracy skills to calculate the financial impact of your solutions. As a result, it is important that you recognise the employability skills that you are developing while completing your academic assignments and solving your daily life challenges.

 example

Do some problem-solving

Need to learn how to think on your feet? It's time to say hello to a voluntary role.

As a leader at your local youth club not only will you be entrusted with the safety of the children, but you may need to resolve misunderstandings between members.

As a charity shop supervisor you could be called upon to address customer concerns or negotiate weekly staff rotas. The beauty of volunteering? Things may not always go to plan but you're sure to be supported by a team of passionate people all working towards the same goal. While it may feel tough at the time, approaching a problem calmly is an important workplace skill that demonstrates your personal resilience and adaptability. Added bonus? Your volunteer experience will leave you ready and raring to go when faced with that old interview chestnut: 'Tell me about a situation where you had to overcome a difficult problem'. To find a voluntary role near you head to Do-it.org, a national volunteering database.

Jamie Ward-Smith, CEO, Do-it.org

Another tool to develop solutions to challenges is the '5 Whys' developed by the Toyota Motor Corporation in 1950. Toyota developed a method where, by repeating 'why' five times, the problem and the solution are revealed through the questioning process. The 5 Whys is used to unveil the root cause of a problem. Once the root has been identified, a solution is developed, which ensures that the problem doesn't reoccur.

It is important through the questioning phase that the key stakeholders are invited to participate in the process, i.e. all those affected by the problem or the situation. Once the team members have been identified, it is important to drill down at least five levels to identify the root cause of the problem, but initially the problem needs to be clearly defined for the process to work.

The five key stages in the 5 Whys process:

1 Identify the key stakeholders – those affected by the problem.

2 Assign a team leader to lead and document the process.

3 Ask 'why' five times.

4 Define the solution and assign responsibilities.

5 Communicate the outcomes with all stakeholders.

brilliant dos and don'ts

What to do and what not to do when problem-solving

✔ Be as specific as possible when thinking and investigating the problem – pinpoint the actual issues using factual information.

✔ Find the most important parts of the problem – what are the biggest issues or risks?

✗ Don't blame others, poor processes or systems for the problem – remain open-minded about the problem and its causes.

✗ Do not immediately assume you know what the problem is and the solutions are.

✗ Do not go straight to solve the problem before thinking, investigating and gathering information about it (facts, inference, speculation and opinion).

Mindmaps can give you an overview of a large subject while also holding large amounts of information. They can be an intuitive way to organise your thoughts, since they mimic the way our brains think – bouncing ideas off of each other, rather than thinking linearly.

Jo Blissett, Career Development Consultant, Career Quest

Communication

Communication in essence is the sending of a message by sender A to receiver B. The format of the message can take different forms and the language will vary dependent on the context. There are several different options available.

Face to face

Despite face to face appearing to be the easiest form of communication, messages can still be misinterpreted by the choice of words, body language, tone and the person delivering the message.

Telephone call

Without the aid of visual expression, the choice of words and tone become even more crucial to ensure the receiver interprets the message accurately. Telephone interviews are often used during the selection process, and students would be advised to practise beforehand, as diction, tone and clarity are paramount.

Written communication

Written communication can take various form, including CVs, reports and covering letters. The style of writing, presentation and choice of words can all affect the way the message is delivered and received.

Social media

Twitter, What'sApp, LinkedIn, Facebook and instant messaging can be misinterpreted due to the incorrect use of upper or lower case, the insertion of an emoticon or an abbreviation. Although an accepted means of communication, it is heavily criticised if not used in the right context.

Effective communication

So how can we communicate effectively? When delivering a message, you need to take into account the context. In what context is the message being delivered? Professional, academic or social. The mode of delivery should reflect the context along with the choice of words.

In addition, to avoid any confusion use the 7Cs of communication

1 **Clear:** Ensure the aim and purpose of your message is clear from the outset of your written or verbal communication.

2 **Concise:** Less is more when communicating so be brief and targeted.

3 **Concrete:** Be focused in your communication and ensure that you are specific, factual and provide the required level of detail.

4 **Correct:** Ensure that your spelling, facts and grammar are correct. Also ensure that the tone, language and choice of words fit the context.

5 **Coherent:** Reread your message to ensure that it is logical and your ideas flow smoothly.

6 **Complete:** Ensure your communication contains the necessary information required by the receiver to respond.

7 **Courteous:** Ensure that you address the recipient politely and appropriately.

(Modified from Cutlip and Center, 1952)

In summary, when communicating you need to understand the context within which the message is to be delivered, that you choose the right medium for delivery and you choose your words carefully. And then use the 7 Cs of communication to avoid any misinterpretation of your message.

Communication skills can be developed through your academic study or extracurricular activities. Academically your presentation skills and written assignments are all opportunities for you to be assessed on how well you communicate. In addition to the academic environment, opportunities will arise to develop communication skills in different contexts. For example, at networking meetings, engaging with student societies or participating in mock interviews. It is important that you are able to communicate in a wide range of contexts including professional, academic and social.

Application of IT

Technology is transforming, disrupting and reshaping all industries. No organisation is insulated from the rapid changes taking place within the technology sector, but it's the resounding ripples and waves that affect all industries as well. The dramatic advances in technology are causing industries to question their purpose in the future. An example of this is the retail banking sector.

'There are so many different ways that you can make payments these days; you can pay by email, by Paypal and you can pay by your mobile phone, but all of that relies on the same plumbing and predominately it's the banks that provide that plumbing. Right now it's of value to us but I think we are in danger of just becoming the plumbing.' (Mortimer, 2015)

Industries are not just facing change – they are facing disruption. As a graduate you will be expected to be IT savvy. Question how technology could improve your processes or add value to your role. Continually update your IT skills, undertake short courses to learn about new technologies and new ways of performing tasks.

The application of IT involves the ability to demonstrate basic IT skills, including the familiarity with word processing, spreadsheets, file management and email. These skills can be developed through completing the assessments on your courses: word processing your coursework, using visual aids for presentations. On campus there will be support classes to develop your IT skills. Extracurricular activities can also be used as a means to develop these skills.

IT skills are essential so don't leave university without them. And make sure you keep them up to date. Course providers, such as UDemy, Coursera or General Assembley, provide short courses to ensure your skills remain current.

Application of numeracy and data analysis

How's your mental maths? Can you analyse data and provide the best course of action? Are you financially literate? When was the last time you calculated an average, percentage or fraction? Well, all of these maths elements can and do feature in selection tests and assessment centres. Numeracy is like Marmite – you either love it or hate it. But either way employers love it.

brilliant definition

Numeracy
'the manipulation of numbers, general mathematical awareness and its application in practical contexts'

CBI, 2011

Numbers are everywhere and underpin many decisions made in organisations, so as a future graduate you need to understand what numeracy means for your sector. Generally, employers will expect you to have an understanding of mental arithmetic tasks like addition, subtraction, multiplication and division. Graduates will also be expected to analyse quantitative and qualitative data, interpret them and present the data in a visual format. You will also need to understand the financial implications of changes in the marketplace on an organisation, their products and profit margins.

Whether you are an arts, law or tourism graduate you need to have basic numeracy skills. Selection processes can include timed mental maths tests, so it's important to refresh these skills before applying to internships or graduate roles.

Practice tests can be found at the following sites:

SHL Direct: www.cebglobal.com

Talentlens: www.talentlens.co.uk

Leadership

Are you a future leader? Are you a game changer? Or are you able to take ownership of a situation and bring it to resolution?

Leadership comes in many forms and varying personalities. There are some excellent examples of leadership in the public arena from Barack Obama to Steve Jobs, but on a daily basis many employees within organisations demonstrate leadership skills.

Organisations need leaders on many levels to drive and champion success throughout a business. Leaders are not only at the helm of an organisation, as in order to be sustainable an organisation needs talented individuals who contribute to its continued success. Graduate schemes develop the pipeline of future leaders within the organisation.

How do we define leadership? As stated by the Chartered Institute of Professional Development (CIPD): 'there is no single definition or concept of leadership that satisfies all'.

Leadership is expected from the CEO right down to the most junior employee. Everyone has their part to play in ensuring excellence is maintained. The CIPD defines leadership as:

'the capacity to influence people, by means of personal attributes and/or behaviours to achieve a common goal'.

This is applicable to the CEO, who has to devise the vision and strategy to the graduate, who joins the organisation and works together with the team to achieve a common goal.

brilliant example

What to do and not do to be an effective leader

- Be yourself: There's no 'right' model for a leader, so don't feel you have to be someone else.

- Know your own strengths and weaknesses: As well as knowing where to improve, you can organise teams to complement your own skills.

- Resist the temptation to 'do it yourself': The best leaders encourage their teams to deliver.

- Define what success looks like: Help people to understand what they are aiming for – the more inspirational the better.

- Don't be afraid to admit when you are wrong: People will respect you more, not less.

What to do and not do when you are leading a task or group

- Be clear on the objective and keep reminding people of it to keep on track.

- Find out what the different strengths of your team members are, and make the most of them.

- Make sure everyone gets some recognition, especially afterwards.

- Don't allow those with the loudest voices to dominate the group. Make sure you involve everyone.

- Don't feel it's all down to you: your job is to get the best from the team not to have the best ideas yourself.

- Don't be afraid to make decisions. Consensus can't always be reached.

John Garnett, Board Advisor, Consultant and former Managing Director

In your graduate application form or the interview you will undoubtedly be asked to provide examples of where you have demonstrated your leadership skills. While at university there are several opportunities for you to develop your skills such as student societies, part-time jobs, volunteering, etc.

Take ownership of a task by developing an action plan of how the goal will be achieved. Employers will be interested in how you approached the task and your learning points. The actual outcome (although a successful one is always good) is immaterial; the way you handle the challenge, plan your time and liaise with others is more important. These will show your ability to lead a team to resolution.

---

brilliant example

The Duke of Edinburgh's Award and leadership skills

Strong leadership skills are developed while doing a DofE programme. As part of a small team, you will plan, practise and complete an expedition. You will have to do a volunteering activity, no doubt taking yourself out of your comfort zone. This will allow you to gain vital leadership skills, whether by encouraging the rest of your expedition group through a particularly tough time, or leading and guiding your local youth group or sports team. The skills developed will be something that you are able to take through life with you, and that will also become invaluable to future employers.

Peter Westgarth, Chief Executive, The Duke of Edinburgh's Award

---

Enterprise

In today's competitive market, regardless of the sector or role that you are recruited into, employers want graduates who are not afraid to disrupt the status quo. The ability to understand and interpret current processes, and how they are interconnected and interrelated, gives rise to opportunities to identify areas for improvement. Being entrepreneurial is not limited to starting your own business; organisations benefit from staff being intrapreneurs, developing new products and processes from within the organisation. This helps to maintain their competitive advantage.

The National Council for Graduate Entrepreneurship (NCGE) states that to add value an entrepreneurial graduate needs to: 'have the entrepreneurial skills that enable them to seize opportunities, solve issues and problems, generate and communicate ideas and make a difference in their communities'.

Students need to seize opportunities where they can be creative and innovative and develop their initiative skills. These can be achieved through involvement with either student societies or small businesses. Both provide opportunities for students to use their initiative to achieve specific goals. In particular, due to small businesses often operating with minimal staff, students can often find that they are exposed to more responsibility within a shorter timescale.

Being entrepreneurial is a must as students need to demonstrate how they will add value to the organisation.

Emotional intelligence

Businesses continually face challenging, demanding and transforming landscapes, and so workforces need to manage and respond accordingly. Companies increasingly realise that the emotional intelligence (EI) of their employees plays an important role in determining an individual's response to a situation or to other people.

As a result, emotional intelligence has become increasingly important when identifying new talent. The leaders of tomorrow need to develop their ability to remain objective and make decisions based on the facts and data related to the situation.

brilliant definition

Emotional intelligence

'Emotional intelligence is the ability to perceive emotions, to access and generate emotions so as to assist thought, to understand emotions and emotional knowledge, and to reflectively regulate emotions so as to promote emotional and intellectual growth'

Mayer & Salovey, 1997, p. 87

Daniel Goleman (2014) identified four key components of an individual's emotional intelligence:

- **Self-awareness:** The ability to recognise how their feelings will affect their job performance.
- **Self-management:** The ability to demonstrate self-control and remain calm and clear-headed even during highly pressured situations.
- **Social awareness:** The ability to listen to what is said and more importantly what is unsaid and allow this to guide both your interaction with others and your decision-making.
- **Relationship management:** Employees with high emotional intelligence have the ability to inspire, influence, develop others, challenge the status quo and manage conflict.

These four elements underpin the ability to perform effectively both within a team and when facing challenging situations within the workplace.

▶ brilliant example

Developing and improving your emotional intelligence

The ability to manage people and relationships is highly regarded by employers, so developing and using your EI can be a great way to show an employer why you stand out in the graduate recruitment market.

Carrying out your own self-evaluation is the first step to developing and improving your EI. You need to look at yourself honestly and identify your strengths and weakness. In addition, you can consider the points and advice in the table below.

Observe how you react to people	Do you stereotype? Do you rush to judge individuals and their actions?	Try to put yourself in their shoes Be more open and accepting of others' views and needs
Examine how you react to stressful situations	Do you become upset if things don't happen the way you want? Do you blame others, even when it's not their fault? Do you allow your emotions to cloud your decisions and thoughts?	Try to demonstrate the ability to stay calm and in control in stressful situations Ensure you keep your emotions in control when things go wrong
Consider how your actions will affect others – before you take action	What will be the impact? How will others feel? Would you want that experience?	Put yourself in their place Identify how you can help others deal with the effects

Jo Blissett, Career Development Consultant, Career Quest

When considering the importance of emotional intelligence, you must also consider resilience, the ability to bounce back following an adverse decision.

brilliant definition

Resilience
'the process of adapting well in the face of adversity, trauma, tragedy, threats or even significant sources of stress'
The American Psychological Association

Having the resolve to continue, whether it be with applications or a challenging situation, is a testament to an individual's character. The graduate market is increasingly competitive in nature, forcing graduates to become more resilient in order to survive. One application is unlikely to result in a positive outcome, and so graduates will receive several rejection letters before securing a graduate position. As a result, resilience is becoming increasingly important to a graduate's success.

There are many opportunities to develop resilience throughout your time at university. For example, a willingness to strive for better grades and to act on feedback from your assignments. In extracurricular activities resilience can be demonstrated by completing challenging tasks such as charity fundraising sky dives, triathlons, marathons, etc.

brilliant example

The Duke of Edinburgh's Award and resilience

Young people are stronger than they think, and the great thing about doing a DofE programme is that it shows them this. Resilience is a work-ready skill, demonstrating that the individual has the capacity to recover quickly from a difficult situation. Learning to put up a tent in all weathers and undertake an expedition in the pouring rain can really test a person. If you can achieve this, many employers will see that you have a trait in you that is gold dust within the workplace.

Peter Westgarth, Chief Executive, The Duke of Edinburgh's Award

brilliant example

Resilience, opportunities and questions

I recognised my need for resilience upon graduation to avoid accepting my immediate reality. I asked myself what my purpose in life was and where I wanted to be. From there I bullet-pointed my answers and set myself deadlines. I looked for opportunities that would push me to my final destination, as opposed to going into a job that had better financial gain but less opportunity for growth.

I became proactive and sought successful people within my field and was not afraid to ask them questions about their routes to success and what barriers they faced. They said: 'Know your strengths and weaknesses, stand out from the crowd and get comfortable being uncomfortable, as when you're comfortable your success is limited'. I took these words and ran with it and each year from 2010 I have achieved something bigger and better.

After university, my full focus was to be the best version of myself within the sporting industry. I soon realised from assessing my strengths and weaknesses along with personal experiences that I had the drive and determination to start my own business. I set up SLR Fitness (personal training) and made many mistakes but learnt from them. I was also told you should not be fearful of failing in aid of wanting to do something you love or wanting to achieve something as it is all a learning curve.

Remember the most valuable stones (diamonds) come out of really dark places so when you feel all the walls are crashing in, do not stay in that dark place, step out and be that shining diamond.

Here are five tips to develop your resilience:

● Get comfortable being uncomfortable.

● Be persistent and do not take NO for an answer.

● Follow up on everything.

● Be opportunity-focused as opposed to money-focused.

● Be around positive, ambitious individuals in a better position than yourself and ask questions.

Stefan Lloyd, SLR Fitness

brilliant recap

● Developing employability skills, competences and attributes underpin the success of today's graduate.

● In 2015 it is estimated that soft skills contribute £88 billion to the UK economy.

● 97% of UK employers believe that soft skills underpin the success of their business and their importance is valued more than academic results.

● 75% of employers have identified a soft skills gap in today's workforce.

● Self-management is your first trial at being a manager.

● The range of challenges faced by organisations require a multitude of skills and expertise to develop a comprehensive solution.

● Business and customer awareness are essential to understand the challenges and opportunities faced by the organisation.

- Organisations continually face challenges and it is important to identify the key stakeholders and collaborate to provide a solution.

- Communication is an essential skill and will underpin the ability to secure a role within an organisation, and to maintain that role.

- Graduates are the future leaders within an organisation.

- Emotional intelligence is just as important as the technical skills an individual brings to an organisation.

CHAPTER 2

Global business needs global graduates

Study abroad is basic training for the 21st century

Institute of International Education

Today's graduates need to understand the challenges of the global market, but more importantly how to identify opportunities. Both private and public-sector organisations can no longer insulate themselves from the impact of the changing global landscape. Graduates need to understand how these changes will impact their discipline and their future industry.

What threats does the global market present? And what opportunities?

Employers need graduates who can navigate the changing global landscape and provide solutions which can guide organisations to continued success. An organisation's survival will be determined by its ability to be enterprising and harness the challenges of change and reinvent them into positive developments. The global graduate is at the heart of this success.

Why we need global graduates

In the twenty-first century graduates will work for organisations that operate in a landscape which has no boundaries and is continually changing, evolving and transforming. Friedman (2005) stated that 'the world is flat'.

Technology has transformed the way we communicate, the way we work and the way we do business. No industry has been able to insulate itself from the digital transformation that technology has brought to each and every industry; those that have tried are no longer with us. Many of the jobs which exist today did not exist ten years ago: from app developers, to cloud computing specialists and from sustainability experts to social media managers.

No aspect of the way we do business has remained the same. From the basics of how we select and pay for goods, to how those goods are transported and delivered. Technology has not only transformed industries, but also levelled the playing field (Friedman, 2007), so that competitors are now no longer the usual suspects.

The challenges posed by both BRIC (Brazil, Russia, China, India) countries and MINT (Mexico, Indonesia, Nigeria, Turkey) countries would be impossible without the transformations which have occurred in the marketplace.

So what does this mean for the twenty-first century graduate? With a backdrop of continual change, companies need graduates who can confidently work in diverse teams and often virtual teams located across the globe. As a result, companies need graduates who will not only help to defend their market but assist with both developing and operating in new markets. (Diamond et al., 2008)

Companies are therefore not limiting their graduate recruitment to national boundaries. Graduates face an increased level of competition, where companies seek to source the best talent with a global perspective.

brilliant tip

Why you should have an international experience

1 Personal development and the opportunity to develop your employability skills.

2 Career opportunities – employers value the skills and attributes gained from students engaging with an international experience.

3 Hone your language skills.

4 Build an international network.

5 It's a life-changing experience.

Despite the importance of an international experience, the data from the Higher Education Statistical Agency (HESA) report on UK Student Mobility do not demonstrate a willingness among UK students to engage with international experiences.

In the academic year of 2014/15 only 1.3% of UK domiciled students undertook an international experience. The rate of adoption by UK students is very low, and not reflective of the level of international students taking advantage of global experiences within the UK Higher Education sector. In 2013 there were 'Nearly 4.3 million students. . .enrolled in University-level education outside their home country'. (OECD, 2013) The UK is one of the second highest destinations of international students globally, but ranks as one of the lowest for sending students abroad, as indicated by the HESA data.

The need for global graduates with a global outlook can be seen in the level of students seeking an international experience. The top five destinations for international students are: United States, United Kingdom, France, Australia and Germany.

Top 20 Destinations For International Students

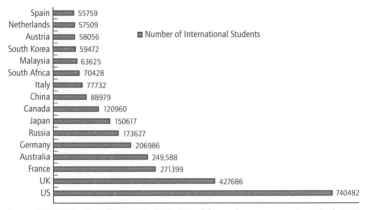

Source: UNESCO Institute for Statistics (UIS), http://www.uis.unesco.org, extracted July 2016

Global competences

Diamond et al. (2008) in a study of 12 graduate recruiters, who represent 3,500 graduate vacancies, identified a list of 'global competencies' which complement the generic employability skills. Regardless of a student's discipline, they would be expected to have generic employability skills as these serve as a baseline for graduates regardless of discipline.

The global competences identified in the study enable students to compete in the global arena. Students who develop these competences will be more able to work in a global capacity participating in global teams.

Employers were asked to rank 14 skills on a scale of 1 to 10, with 1 being the least important and 10 being the most important (and no number was to be used twice). This left four competences scoring zero. The findings of the ranking are listed below.

1   An ability to work collaboratively with teams of people from a range of backgrounds and countries.

2   Excellent communication skills: both speaking and listening.

3   A high degree of drive and resilience.

4   An ability to embrace multiple perspectives and challenge thinking.

5   A capacity to develop new skills and behaviours according to role requirements.

6   A high degree of self-awareness.

7   An ability to negotiate and influence clients across the globe from different cultures.

8   An ability to form professional, global networks.

9   An openness to and respect for a range of perspectives from around the world.

10 Multi-cultural learning agility.

11 Multi-lingualism.

12 Knowledge of foreign economies and own industry area overseas.

13 An understanding of one's position and role within a global context or economy.

14 A willingness to play an active role in society at a local, national and international level.

---

brilliant example

Volunteering in Uganda

I spent the most amazing summer as an International Citizens Service (ICS) volunteer in Uganda. It was a heart-warming, eye-opening and life-changing time where I not only gained perspective on my work (and life) but also gained a new family for life by staying with a Ugandan host family.

The programme allowed me to work with seven entrepreneurs with businesses ranging from a sugar cane farm to selling cosmetics. I worked with them to launch their exciting and innovative businesses to create jobs and improve their lives. As part of my action at home, I currently have the responsibility of selecting the UK volunteers who wish to take part in ICS.

Hermon Amanuel, BA in Business and Enterprise

So how will students develop these skills and do you need to go overseas to develop them? 'Success is all in the global mindset'. (Govindarajan and Gupta 1998)

A global mindset instantly means that you are open to new ideas, willing to step out of your comfort zone, but ultimately curious about the world we live in and the people within it. Alongside the ability to develop a global mindset is the cultural agility and cultural dexterity to adapt your style of working to reflect that of the culture and customs within the country you are operating within.

'I think cultural dexterity is important: an ability not to impose one's own culture on another one, to be sensitive to other cultures and how to do business in different environments. There are certain ways of working with clients in the Middle East that you wouldn't adopt in Japan. (PwC) (Diamond et al., 2008, p. 9)

Central to the global mindset is the need for adaptability in every aspect of the way you work. If you are truly a global graduate, this will be reflected in the way you communicate in an international context.

Naturally you will be mindful of customs and demonstrate a level of understanding when operating in different countries. There is an acceptance that a diverse team is needed to secure an outcome which is globally acceptable and globally competitive. Operating in various countries around the world requires a certain level of flexibility, but an abundance of resilience. There is a definite willingness to go with the flow and accept a different way of doing things. As they say 'When in Rome, do as the Romans do'. In order to appreciate and fully develop solutions, which work on a global basis, it's important to fully immerse yourself into the culture to understand the challenges and the opportunities which exist.

To gauge the level of opportunity in any of the countries in which organisations operate requires a level of knowledge about global affairs. Reimers (2011) stated that commercial and business awareness for the global graduate is 'not just at one country level but at a global level'.

Global decisions are underpinned by a knowledge and awareness of the market which informs the decision-making process at every level. Graduates will be required to understand their industry on a local, national and international basis. Companies operating within this landscape with reduced boundaries need to understand where the next threat will come from or where opportunities are opening. Knowledge is at the heart of global success.

brilliant example

Have an international experience

The benefits of an international experience – be it studying abroad or combining an international work placement with studying – are well documented. A number of recent studies have re-emphasised the benefits of international experience to students in terms of boosting employability prospects, starting salaries and academic achievement.

The latest Gone International report by the Higher Education International Unit (HEIU, 2016) found that unemployment rates for students six months after graduation were lower among internationally mobile students at 5%, compared with 7% for their non-mobile peers. Black and Asian students seemed to benefit the most from international experience, with their employment prospects showing the biggest improvement: 9.9% of non-mobile, black graduates were unemployed six months after graduation, compared to 5.4% of black, mobile graduates. The corresponding data for Asian students showed that unemployment fell to 4.4% for Asian, mobile students, compared with 9.5% for Asian, non-mobile graduates.

The report also found that employed graduates who had engaged in international experience were more likely (74.8%) than their non-mobile peers (67.1%) to gain employment within one of the top three socio-economic classifications.

Mobile students across almost all socio-economic backgrounds reported higher average salaries than their non-mobile peers. The average salary of a mobile student six months after graduation was £21,349 (compared to £20,519 for a non-mobile student).

The European Commission's Erasmus Impact Study (EIS, 2016) analyses the longer-term impact of mobility on career progression and revealed that former Erasmus students are half as likely to experience long-term unemployment compared to those without international experience.

Students in eastern Europe slashed their risk of long-term unemployment by 83% by taking part in Erasmus (European Commission, 2016). The positive employability impact existed even five to ten years after graduation, where the unemployment rate of mobile students was lower than that of non-mobile students. In particular, work placements were found to have a direct positive impact on employability, with one in three Erasmus students being offered employment by their host company.

Another interesting aspect of the study was the inclusion of personality trait tests for students before and after mobility. The approach looked at six 'memo© factors' that are seen as key employability traits. Ninety-three percent of employers surveyed confirmed that these six traits were key to the recruitment and professional development of employees. Erasmus students from all regions showed higher values for the six personality traits than non-mobile students, even prior to going abroad. Moreover, the mobility experience itself enhanced these traits, boosting the already existing advantage of Erasmus students over non-mobiles by a further 40%.

Here are some ways to overcome barriers to international experience:

- Research funding opportunities: Erasmus mobility grants are available to EU students (https://www.britishcouncil.org/study-work-create/opportunity/study-abroad/erasmus).

- Research scholarships at your university: You may find funding is available for flights or other expenditure linked to mobility.

- Consider a year abroad: This is typically heavily subsidised with students paying just 15 to 20% of annual fees.

- Consider a short international experience: This could be an international summer school. For example, the British Council website has information on short courses (https://www.britishcouncil.org/study-work-create/ opportunity/study-abroad).

- Consider combining study abroad with an international work placement: You can seek assistance from companies such as InternshipGuru (www. internshipGuru.co.uk) that facilitate overseas work placements.

Karen St Jean-Kufuor, Principal Lecturer, Westminster Business School

Becoming a global graduate

So how do you become a global graduate? CIHE (2008) found that 29% of employers discovered that students were more employable once they had engaged with an opportunity to study overseas. As a result, the UK is challenged in that only 1.3% of the total UK domicile undergraduate students undertake international experiences, and so the opportunity to be fully immersed in an international culture is not sought after by UK students.

On the other hand, as the UK is the second highest destination for international learners, it enables UK students to develop their cultural sensitivity by learning side by side with international students. Despite this opportunity, it still does not outweigh the benefit of the experience of having to adapt to living in a different culture.

brilliant recap

- Global businesses need global graduates.
- Technology has transformed the way we do business.
- No industry has been able to insulate itself from change.
- Competitors are no longer the usual suspects.

- Only 1.3% of UK domiciled students undertake student mobility.

- The top four global competences are collaboration, communication, drive and resilience and an ability to adopt multiple perspectives and challenge thinking.

- Employers value students who have had an international experience.

- Knowledge about international markets underpin global decision-making.

- A global mindset instantly states you are open to new ideas, willing to step out of your comfort zone, and are ultimately curious about the world we live in and the people within it.

CHAPTER 3

Employability in and out of the lecture theatre

Businesses look first and foremost for graduates with the right attitudes and aptitudes to enable them to be effective in the workplace – nearly nine in ten employers (89%) value these above factors such as degree subject (62%).

CBI, 2015

f 72% of students are graduating with a 2:1 or a first (HESA, 2015), you cannot rely on your degree to make you stand out. Your extracurricular activities and your work experience will be the focus of most employers.

In order to truly benefit from your time at university and leave with more than just a degree, students need to recognise the skills employers value. Generic employability skills are core to all graduates regardless of discipline. Employers have an expectation that when they recruit a graduate, their ability and aptitude to demonstrate employability skills is a foregone conclusion.

In many cases a degree is merely the passport for entry. It is the demonstration of employability skills that is used to differentiate candidates. These skills are built into the curriculum and can be further developed through participation in extracurricular activities.

The first step for students is to understand what is meant by employability and the skills valued by employers. The second stage is to recognise these skills within the curriculum and how they can be gained through extracurricular activities.

This chapter highlights the ways in which universities attempt to embed employability into the curriculum, but also how students can take charge of their own development of employability skills utilising extracurricular activity both on and off campus.

What do employers want?

Employability is a key priority for employers when recruiting graduates. A report entitled 'Inspiring Growth: CBI/Pearson Education and Skills Survey' stated:

A degree allows you to enter the arena, but it is the ability to develop relevant employability skills that will differentiate you from the competition and help you secure a graduate position. Students who are able to communicate the relevance of the skills developed throughout their degree and those developed through extracurricular activities to the world of work will be the most successful.

The report highlights the top three factors that employers focus on when selecting graduates:

● Attitude and aptitude (88%).
● Relevant work experience or industry placement (67%).
● Degree subject (62%).

A positive can-do attitude is paramount. In challenging times the workplace needs employees who can rise to the challenge, provide inspiration and be innovative. Students must seek opportunities either in their work experience, extracurricular or voluntary activities to demonstrate their ability to be flexible and positive in their approach to challenging tasks. Students should also seek opportunities which demonstrate their willingness to opt in: to step outside their comfort zone.

If you need examples of these activities, think about what you dread most and that's probably the activity you need to do. For instance, if you fear presentations take on a role which forces you to make them, or if you have not experienced another culture apart from on a family holiday, take on an overseas volunteering opportunity.

The report also says: 'Businesses are primarily focused on what individual graduates can bring to the workplace'.

Work experience

Work experience has become an important factor when competing in the graduate job market. Employers want to see how you cope in a live environment, putting your skills to the test.

The High Fliers Report 2016 reinforces the importance of work experience. More than 50% of *The Times'* top 100 graduate employers stated: 'that it was either "not very likely" or "not at all likely" that a graduate who'd had no previous work experience at all with any employers would be successful during their selection process and be made a job offer, irrespective of their academic achievements or the university they attended'.

This statement is very significant as students cannot postpone finding work experience opportunities until after graduation. In fact, the more experiences the better. Students should be actively seeking to secure opportunities during summer breaks and other holidays.

Many companies actively provide opportunities for students to engage with them. According to the High Fliers Report, within the top 100 companies alone 90% provide paid work experience opportunities, and this does not include the remainder of the blue chip companies, small and medium-sized enterprises or third-sector organsiations. Two-fifths of the top 100 companies also provide opportunities to engage in introductory courses, open day and taster experiences for first-year students.

The importance of the degree subject studied only becomes of more significant value when considering careers in manufacturing, science and engineering. Among these sectors the importance of the degree subject studied was 80% (CBI/Pearson, 2015). The Inspiring Growth Report also highlighted that 40% of employers preferred

STEM subjects for the rigour of mathematical and analytical skills. These skills are in high demand in the business sector.

Commercial awareness

Commercial awareness is continually stated as a concern of employers, in particular during the interview process. Both Targetjobs and Prospects list this as one of the skills that graduates need to ensure they develop while at university. As Targetjobs states: 'It's how the industry fits together'.

We currently live in an age where information is literally at our fingertips. Students therefore have no excuse on why they might not be abreast of developments occurring within their preferred industry. This is even more of an issue when students attend interviews and simply have not taken the time to research the company, their competitors or the industry.

Targetjobs highlights the following as the minimum level of commercial awareness required by a graduate:

- Understanding of the key competitors and their position in the market.
- An ability to converse confidently about market trends and speculate about the future.
- Knowledge of historical or cyclical trends which have shaped the marketplace.

The importance and relevance of employability skills will continue to increase and will become the determinant of graduates' success. As stated above, academic results pale into insignificance when compared to students' development of employability skills.

Why are these skills important?

Regardless of your discipline, career choice or preferred industry sector, these skills underpin your success. Whether you're an arts, engineering or chemistry graduate, you will need to produce reports, find solutions to business problems and communicate effectively with customers, management or colleagues. The development of these skills is paramount to your success. They represent the foundation of the skills required to succeed in the workplace. The table below shows how these skills are used in the work environment.

Employability skill	Relevance to the workplace
Team-working	When you join an organisation you will undoubtedly become part of a team, so your ability to work with others and to perform within the group becomes an important skill set. Your ability to participate and add value to your team is essential.
Leadership	The ability to demonstrate leadership skills, to take ownership of a task and be able to negotiate, influence and be assertive in your approach to secure a positive outcome. Leadership skills are required by all who have responsibility within an organisation.
Positive attitude	Underpinning a positive attitude is viewing the glass as half-full as opposed to half-empty. Positive energy and a willingness to be open to new ideas and alternative solutions will enable you to develop creative solutions to challenges in the workplace.
Communication	Communication, both verbal and written, is an essential requirement for graduate roles. The ability to communicate both to internal and external customers is paramount. Accuracy in your written work is a must, and confidence and clarity when speaking in meetings and on the telephone is essential.
Problem-solving	The ability to analyse, critically evaluate and formulate a solution are essential skills. Graduates will be expected to be able to demonstrate critical thinking and analytical skills via their academic study or through their work experience.

(continued)

Employability skill	Relevance to the workplace
Numeracy	The ability to engage with numbers and support your arguments with hard facts and figures adds to the validity of decisions or proposed solutions. Accuracy and the ability to analyse numerical data is a must.
Cultural sensitivity	Organisations rely heavily on their ability to not only attract a diverse workforce, but also to interact on a global scale with diverse audiences. As a result, the need to be culturally aware is highly valued in an international company.
Commercial	Understanding the environment within which a business operates will add to your effectiveness, as you will have an understanding of not only the challenges faced by the organisation but also the opportunities presented by the changing landscape.

Are universities responsible for the development of employability skills?

The Robbins report (1963) argued that universities were tasked with 'instructing students in skills suitable to play a part in the general division of labour'. This idea was further compounded by the Dearing report (1997, para. 1.1), which placed higher education as central to the 'development of our people, our society, and our economy . . . In the next century, the economically successful nations will be those which become learning societies: where all are committed, through effective education and training, to lifelong learning'.

More recently in 2010, David Willets, UK Minister of State for Universities and Science, called for universities 'to provide public statements on what they do to promote employability, to encourage them to improve the job-readiness of their students and to do better at getting their students into internships, work experience and work'.

Today the focus is more a collaboration between businesses and universities to identify the skills gap to ensure students are developing the skills needed to maintain the UK's competitive edge. The UK Commission for Employment and Skills in 2013 stated that one in five vacancies remain unfilled due to lack of skills, qualifications or experience. Businesses need to work closer with universities to make sure the right skills are being developed.

🔍 **brilliant** Impact

How universities enhance employability skills

Many universities now seek to attract students by promising to enhance their employability skills. This is logical, given that many students now see themselves as investing in their human capital through their tuition fees. Given this promise and this expectation, it is vital that such institutions deliver what they say, and actually do enhance their students' employability skills.

But how? To some extent, such development should come naturally from undergraduate study. The ability to think critically, to master information and to communicate the results of research should all be developed at university. But other employability skills, equally valuable at work – such as teamwork and problem-solving – are less obviously relatable to traditional academic study. And even when such skills should emerge from higher education, if they are not developed alongside a growing commercial awareness, they may not readily transfer to employment.

This is why it is vital that higher education institutions work with the businesses their students will work for, to embed employability skills systematically in the curriculum. From course design and development; to the student experience in the classroom; to assessment of the knowledge and skills learned; and to internships and placements during study, business should be involved at every stage of the process in any higher education experience that purports to enhance employability skills.

Ben Hughes, Vice Principal (academic delivery),

Pearson Business School

Universities clearly have a role to play in providing and developing a highly skilled workforce, but the onus is clearly not just on them. Businesses have a role to play in defining the skills needed for the future in order to compete, but in order for universities to translate these skills into the curriculum there is a need for collaboration. Businesses are also required to provide opportunities for students to develop their skills in a live environment.

To what degree do students have to take responsibility for the development of their employability skills? In a position paper on employability in 2011, the Association of Graduate Careers Advisory Services advised students to 'take responsibility for [their] own employability'. Students must actively engage with their academic studies and the development of their employability skills.

The table below shows the employment rates of the top five UK universities for graduate job prospects.

The top five universities for graduate job prospects	Employment rate (%)
St George's University of London	93.4
Imperial College London	91.1
University of Cambridge	89.3
University of Oxford	87.1
University of Birmingham	86.7
Source: Times Higher Education, 21 September 2015	

While at university, students will be presented with opportunities to further develop their employability through extracurricular activities.

Employability in the curriculum

All too often, where employability is embedded in the curriculum, students do not readily make the connection between their learning and the world of work. This section reviews some of the assessment methods adopted by subject areas to ensure students develop valuable skills required in the workplace.

Other examples of employability in the curriculum are the use of placements, where students are allocated credits for undertaking a work placement, usually for a set duration, typically a year. Increasingly, companies are collaborating with universities to develop industry days or workshops to provide students with an insight into how their business works. It is also a good opportunity for companies to engage with students and identify potential talent. Students should always ensure that they are engaged and do their research on any company due to attend their university.

Many degrees often include the opportunity for study abroad, usually for one semester or term. This can greatly enhance a student's cultural awareness, a skill desired by global organisations.

With all the above, universities can provide students with a plethora of opportunities to enhance their employability, but how and if they engage with these opportunities is dependent upon the student.

Assessment method	Transferable skills
Group assignments	Students are often required to work in teams to complete a group task. Students develop project management, team-building, negotiation and influencing skills, all highly relevant to the world of work.
Presentations	The ability to develop a well-structured presentation that communicates the key points effectively and efficiently is a valuable skill, useful in a variety of situations beyond a degree.
Case-study analysis	Case-study analysis presents a business scenario and requires students to utilise critical thinking, analytical and problem-solving skills not only to identify the key challenges, but also to make recommendations drawing on both the internal and external environments faced by the organisation. Case studies are often used within the selection process to differentiate candidates.

(continued)

Assessment method	Transferable skills
Report writing	Accuracy and clarity in report writing is a must. Literacy skills are central to academic studies and for application forms and writing reports or emails in the workplace.
Problem-based learning	The ability to resolve problems and provide well-founded solutions is directly transferable to the workplace, where students will be continually presented with challenges.
Research	Research skills are applicable to all industries. The ability to collate, synthesise, analyse and clearly present information found can add value to all organisations, whether private, public or third-sector. All industries are reliant upon information to provide insights into current industry dynamics, future trends and possible opportunities and threats in the marketplace.
Personal development planning	PDP encourages reflection on strengths and weaknesses and develops self-awareness, which supports continual development and learning.
Examinations	Examinations present the opportunity to apply an understanding to scenarios or questions within a time constraint. Many professions use professional examinations to test candidates' knowledge and application of the subject matter. An ability to pass examinations is a required skill within the workplace.

Employability and extracurricular activities

University presents students with an opportunity to experience a whole host of new experiences, from running a society to voluntary work, but you have to make the decision to get involved. Often students will say 'But I don't have time'. My answer to you is *make* time. We all have periods in our days where we think 'Where did the time go?'

Dedicating time to extracurricular activities is an investment in you. There is so much to be gained that you can't afford to miss out. It is these aspects of your time at university that help you to stand out upon graduation. You will have a wider pool of experiences to talk about than just your academic studies, not to mention your self-development from taking part in these activities.

Getting involved in extracurricular activities also speaks volumes about your character. It shows an employer that you have initiative, energy and lots of get up and go. Here is a range of opportunities that you can get involved with from day one at university.

The students' union

The students' union is an opportunity to develop employability skills while having fun. You can either join an existing society or create your own. A freshers' fair is held at the beginning of the academic year and it is an opportunity for existing societies to showcase to new students, but also to recruit new members.

Often students sign up at the freshers' fair but don't become actively involved. Students should seize this opportunity to become active within the society to help organise events and network with students from different courses and various faculties. You can also put into practice many of the skills learnt on your course. For example, event management students could manage, market and budget events, while IT students develop websites and create member databases. The possibilities are endless, but it all starts with a willingness to get involved.

The opportunities presented by the students' union are not limited to the university: every university has a union so there are also opportunities to collaborate. You can develop degree-related and self-development skills, which enhance confidence and make great talking points at interviews. There is no limit to the opportunities presented by being involved in the students' union: the only limiting factor is you.

![brilliant] action

Get involved with your students' union

Employers are always looking for the candidate who stands out from the rest. Across the country, in students' unions and common rooms, thousands of students are involved in a variety of activities. They're playing sport, running societies, campaigning, supporting other students and helping to organise projects.

Whether students are involved in one aspect of university life or multiple, their skills are evident when I meet them. NUS has worked with the Confederation of British Industry to catalogue the skills students develop by engaging in their students' unions. The range is huge, including learning how to handle budgets, leading groups of students, gaining campaigning skills, building teams, supporting new students and communicating effectively.

By getting involved in your students' union you'll be able to explore your passions, meet new friends and build skills. Not only will you become that 'stand out' candidate, but your time at university will be more fulfilling as well.

Megan Dunn, President of the National Union of Students

University societies

The majority of societies have a range of either elected or appointed posts: president of the society, treasurer, marketing officer, event co-ordinator. Employers are impressed by students who can demonstrate the skills to run a society successfully as it builds a range of skills.

- **Leadership skills:** You don't have to be the president of a society to develop leadership skills. Taking ownership of a task or role and demonstrating the ability to influence, negotiate for resources and motivate others to achieve a common goal are all examples of leadership qualities. These skills will resonate with an employer, as part of an organisation's goal is to identify people who have the ability to lead or manage a team.

- **Project management:** Whether you are at university or in the workplace, you will always need to have a clear plan of action on how you will achieve your goals. The ability to plan, adhere to deadlines, identify key milestones and to succeed are all part of the organisational skills required within the work environment.

- **Event management:** The co-ordination and planning involved in a successful event demonstrates your ability to multi-task and strong organisational skills. Event management requires a high level of organisational skills, from liaising with speakers and developing and distributing the marketing communication to negotiating additional resources. The ability to co-ordinate a successful event is an impressive addition to your CV. The busy workplace will always require the ability to multi-task, while maintaining standards. Organisational skills and the ability to meet deadlines are musts for successful graduates.

- **Budgeting:** The ability to budget and forecast demonstrates an understanding of how decisions will affect the bottom line. For instance, understanding how to budget for the costs associated with an event and balance these costs in relation to ticket sales to break even or make a profit are valuable skills. All organisations will value these skills, and will especially value your ability to highlight the relationship between decision-making and the impact on costs, as the economy requires all industries to operate efficiently. These skills are directly transferable to all industry sectors.

- **Communication:** Both written and spoken communication can be developed in participation in a society and their value is transferable to the workplace. The ability to write a persuasive email or report (for example, requesting support for the society) or the development of effective marketing materials (for instance, providing members with updates and information) are useful skills. Employers will expect a high standard of literacy and communication skills. You will be required to produce reports, communicate with clients and provide information to other departments in the organisation.

● **Networking:** Networking will help the enterprising student to secure additional resources for their society, engage the services of speakers and professionals for a reduced fee and meet individuals from different backgrounds and interests. Networking is the backbone of all business. The ability to maintain a wide network is useful not only for university but also to identify possible opportunities.

As a result, you can develop valuable skills on campus and you can decide how you manage your time in relation to your studies. Joining and becoming active in your union is a great way to build practical examples of your skills for future application forms. The other often overlooked skill involved in joining a society is your ability to self-manage. Your decisions and actions are all self-directed and speak volumes about your ability to manage and influence others.

---

brilliant example

President of Leicester African and Caribbean Society

Being the President of Leicester African and Caribbean Society has allowed me to develop skills that are transferable to my future career. This role has provided me with the opportunity to experience university in a different way. These skills and attributes range from confidence, decision-making and teamwork to interpersonal skills. I developed these skills through the planning of events, delegating of tasks and general running of the society.

It has given me new opportunities I would not have had, had I not been in this position, from establishing external links through sponsoring education opportunities and recruitment networking and conference events with large corporations, to creating links with students from different courses and universities.

It has broadened both my professional and social network. I have also been able to embrace diversity on a larger scale, being a society with a plethora of cultures, allowing me to try and experience new things.

Damilola Anderson, President,
Leicester African and Caribbean Society

Voluntary work

When I mention voluntary work, often the first response from students is: 'I can't afford to work for free'. With increasing student debt and the rising cost of living, no one would expect you to give up paid part-time work, but even if you just volunteer for an hour a week, by the end of the year you would have donated 52 hours of voluntary work.

Before deciding to get involved, students should assess their existing commitments and be realistic about the amount of time they have to offer. Volunteers provide valuable support to charities and organisations and so there has to be a certain level of commitment.

Complete the following time assessment to review how much time you have available to volunteer. Enter details of your classes, home study, part-time work, any sports or other commitments. This will highlight what time you can devote to volunteering.

	Monday	Tuesday	Wednesday	Thursday	Friday	Saturday	Sunday
9.00							
10.00							
11.00							
12.00							
13.00							
14.00							
15.00							
16.00							
17.00							
18.00							
19.00							

Volunteering provides a wide range of opportunities for students to undertake and develop an array of skills. Organisations recognise that the relationship represents a win–win situation as they benefit from the additional resource that volunteers represent; and students gain opportunities for self-development and a chance to experience various career options. The greatest benefit of volunteering is the sense of achievement. By giving even just an hour a week you can make a difference to an individual, a community or an organisation.

brilliant example

Be a volunteer

Calling all students. Volunteering isn't just good for the soul; it can also put you on track to improve your career. Volunteering is a way to develop new skills, give a healthy boost to your self-confidence and show future employers you've got drive and initiative. If you're keen to get started, head over to Do-it.org, the UK's largest volunteering database. With over 1.4 million places available for you to choose from it's a great place to start looking.

Whether you choose to work in the private, voluntary or public sector, volunteering can set you apart from other candidates when applying for jobs. Employers are increasingly looking for people who have challenged and stretched themselves beyond their degree course and voluntary experience will help you to shine.

Don't be put off if organisations you are interested in cannot accommodate you. Some don't have the resources to manage volunteers, but there are always others to try. Do-it.org has the widest range of available opportunities, but if you'd prefer to speak to someone directly about volunteer roles in your area, find your local volunteer centre or have a chat with your university's careers service.

If you want to volunteer to help boost your career, think carefully about the skills and experience you need. Volunteering can help you understand the world of work, inspire a future career path and provide you with a solid reference. Don't be afraid to be upfront about this when you apply for opportunities. Volunteering can be a great chance to try different things and, as long as you show commitment, most organisations will welcome the fact that it could have knock-on benefits for you.

Whatever you want to achieve through volunteering, the basic advice is the same: find a volunteering opportunity that really interests you. You might be volunteering with a big national organisation or a small local one, and it might be the cause that excites you or the specific role. You will still get much more out of giving your time if it is something you really want to do.

Jamie Ward-Smith, CEO, Do-it.org

From an employer's perspective, a candidate who can demonstrate a willingness to help others and give up their time represents the kind of person that many organisations would like to recruit. Both public- and private-sector organisations have objectives related to corporate social responsibility and often encourage employees to get involved with volunteering initiatives.

The benefits of volunteering are far-reaching for both the volunteer and the beneficiary. Additional examples of volunteering possibilities include the Duke of Edinburgh's Award.

brilliant example

The Duke of Edinburgh's Award and volunteering

The DofE Award is widely known as the world's leading youth achievement award, with over 300,000 young people currently doing their DofE in the UK every year. Over three award levels – bronze, silver and gold – there is the opportunity to learn and develop skills that will be invaluable throughout life and will open doors to work. Achieving a DofE Award demonstrates that a young person is willing to commit, is driven and determined. This lays a great path for their future, fostering a work ethic and attitude that many employers look for in applicants.

Other work-ready skills that young people develop doing their DofE come from being pushed out of their comfort zones and facing new and exciting challenges. While each young person chooses their own skill to learn, physical goal to achieve, volunteering activity to do and expedition aim (and for gold a residential purpose), the common framework of a programme is structured to develop vital skills and characteristics needed to succeed in life, such as team-working, communication and resilience. An added and important benefit is that young people can demonstrate that they have these skills when applying for jobs and at interviews.

Claire Miles, Managing Director, UK Customer Operations, British Gas, says: 'The DofE develops the skills we look for in our employees like initiative and a determination to learn and progress. It also helps our new recruits to relate to our customers and their lives through the time they spend volunteering in the community – vitally important in a customer-focused business like ours'.

Here are five reasons to start your DofE:

● The DofE gives you the chance to try something completely new and improve on things you are already doing.

- It takes you out of your comfort zone and into a place where you'll push yourself and have amazing new experiences.
- You'll build confidence, resilience, skills and friendship groups – all while having fun.
- It is completely personal to you, with a common framework, meaning it can support you in developing vital skills to help you succeed in life and work.
- The DofE can help to carve out a better future. Employers regard a DofE award very highly.

Peter Westgarth, Chief Executive,
The Duke of Edinburgh's Award

Enterprise opportunities

Have you got what it takes to run your own business? University provides an excellent environment to start your own business. Most universities provide training and support for students to explore business ideas, through academic study or extracurricular activities. Facebook and Dell were both started at university and then expanded upon.

Do you have an idea you want to explore? Now is the time to do it as there are experienced advisers willing to provide support. Universities will often have an enterprise centre to support and develop your idea as well as help you start your own business. There are also a number of organisations ready to support student entrepreneurs to start their own business.

brilliant example

The National Association of College and University Entrepreneurs

The National Association of College and University Entrepreneurs (NACUE) is one of the UK's leading organisations for engaging students in enterprise, set up by students for students. The idea was formed in 2008 by 12 enterprise ▷

society presidents who were already playing a leading role in the development of student entrepreneurship at their institutions. They realised that together they could create something bigger.

Those original 12 societies were catalysts for an extraordinary movement in student entrepreneurship. That initial group has grown into a national non-profit organisation and a thriving national network representing 260 college and university enterprise societies. NACUE is still a passionate advocate for the enterprise society model, as it enables students to practise entrepreneurship in a safe environment, gaining the valuable soft skills needed to thrive in a competitive job market.

Enterprise societies come in all shapes and sizes. Some provide funding, business incubator space and pop-up shops for student start-ups, while others run 'hackathons' to create solutions to business problems, bring leading speakers to campuses, and even create policy thinktanks.

NACUE also champions the need for students to connect, share ideas and network with like-minded peers. It achieves this by hosting a variety of national and regional events, such as the Student Enterprise Conference that brings hundreds of students together for an energising weekend of talks, workshops and networking. It also hosts an annual Leaders Summit that brings together enterprise society committees to share their achievements from the year.

CEO Johnny Luk, National Association of
College and University Entrepreneurs

While at university test your business ideas. Conduct the market research and see whether your idea is really viable. Your university campus represents a good opportunity to conduct this research, with between 20,000 and 30,000 students this is a great opportunity to see if it is a winning idea.

Investigate the level of support offered by your university to start your business while you are still studying. Universities offer not only support while you are a student but also the opportunity to join an incubator upon graduation. There is a range of resources before a start-up and for start-up businesses. There are also a variety of organisations that provide support to start-ups. For instance, Google Campus in London provides, support, networking and mentoring opportunities.

Before students commence on this journey, the first question to ask is 'do you have what it takes to be an entrepreneur?' Being an entrepreneur requires great determination: the ability to face numerous challenges and still have the resolve to start all over again the next day.

Risk-taking is an inherent part of starting a business. The path is not smooth and paved with gold. On the contrary, the road is rough and lined with thorns, but if you are able to survive the journey the rewards and the sense of accomplishment are priceless.

Essential to developing your business idea is building your network and developing relationships. Your ability to connect with people and your likeability become an important factor in the success of your business.

brilliant tip

Levi's top ten roots of success

Levi Roots is a successful entrepreneur, chef musician, author and speaker. If you have a business idea, use these tips to explore your ideas further while you are at university:

1   **Feel the power of your passion:** You will need passion for your business idea, as you will face many challenges along the way, but it is your passion that will propel you forward to your success.

2   **To succeed you must know your market:** Knowledge is key. Do your research about your product, your market and your potential consumers.

Levi Roots Entrepreneur, Chef, Musician, Author and Speaker

▶

3 **The plan is your key to success:** Nelson Mandela said: 'It always seems impossible until it's done'. It is important to plan your journey, so that you arrive at your final destination.

4 **Find yourself a mentor:** Mentors can help you navigate some of the pitfalls of business and provide you with invaluable support and guidance.

5 **Make yourself and your business special:** What's your unique selling point? Whether you are selling a business idea or applying for a job, you need to stand out from the crowd.

6 **Never be afraid to make mistakes:** Mistakes are inevitable but don't make the same mistake twice.

7 **Surround yourself with like-minded people:** Build a network or people who not only challenge you, but complement your skill set.

8 **Focus on finances:** Look after the pennies and the pounds will look after themselves. The ability to budget is a valuable skill both in business and in life.

9 **Stay true to your values and yourself.** Be brave, be passionate, be confident, but never lose sight of who you are.

10 **Be in it for the long term:** Nelson Mandela also said: 'A winner is a dreamer, who never gives up'. Believe in your own magic and don't let anyone tell you any different!

Finally, Levi says: 'Your future success depends upon the strength of your self-belief and the choices that you make'.

Levi Roots, Entrepreneur, Levi Roots

A future strategy that can help you sell your business for a million pounds is worth planning. Here are business leader Yvonne Thompson's seven steps.

brilliant tip

Seven steps to a seven-figure exit based on the seven Ps

Passion: If you want to achieve something great, you need to have passion in your heart. Your hard work and commitment combined with this passion is sure to lead you to success.

Product: The product needs to be in a position to attract the potential buyers. It must be unique and matchless but be careful not to work on something that is too specialised or difficult.

People: A company or a business is nothing without people. You need to have a strong management team along with passionate and experienced employees.

Preparation: A considerable amount of preparation is required for the most successful seven-figure exit. The more you focus on this step, the more likely it is for you to have a rewarding exit.

Pipeline: Pipelining involves different stages in which you show the opportunities, do research, compile data and go on with the proposals.

Promote: What can be more tempting for potential buyers other than some attractive promotions? You need to carefully target your audience and follow a proper strategy to inspire customers.

Post-success: The last P is the prayer. Do not underestimate the power of prayer as it is a sure-fire way to help you find a successful seven-figure exit.

Dr Yvonne Thompson, CBE, Author,
Marketing Guru and International Public Speaker

And here are more tips on developing a business idea.

Five top tips on developing a business idea

1 It's important to pick a business that you believe can gain traction. Ideally it should be an issue that you are passionate about and believe to be commercially viable, as well as important to solve.

2 An idea is just that . . . an idea until you develop and execute it.

3 Be clear about your potential market. Keep revisiting your plans and keep your focus on your market . . . and keep confirming who that market is.

4 Research your sector and explore how you might disrupt it.

5 Be prepared to put your own money into your start-up.

Denise Rabor, Founder of WOW Beauty
and Leadership3sixty

Many students use their talents to support themselves during their time at university. Their goal may not be to start their own business, but the attraction is working for themselves and being able to decide their own rate of pay and hours. So review your skill set. Do you have a skill that you could use to earn money?

Employers need employees who have an entrepreneurial spirit. To run a business while at university demonstrates creativity, initiative and ability. Students have given piano lessons, tutored students in maths and English, built websites, etc. Obviously you need to be proficient in your skill first, but it sounds impressive that you ran your own business while at university.

brilliant example

Creating Yaantu

Yaantu was created after attending a number of 'industry days' at Pearson College (students descend on a business to learn about the problems it faces and work with it to develop solutions). Having noticed the growing need for businesses to have a positive impact on the world, a small team of students began to develop a solution that combined this with our passion for wearable tech with corporate social responsibility. The solution allows employees to track their exercise using a variety of wearables and apps, and in return the employer supports a charity of the employees' choice.

Starting a business has been one of the hardest things I have done to date, with lesson number one being that you make your own luck. We quickly learnt that selling business to business (B2B) is about developing and working your network. Pearson was immensely helpful with setting up sales meetings and off the back of these we won our first customers.

Starting Yaantu while at university had its downsides (juggling workloads and sacrificing a few Friday night beers), but the upsides hugely outweigh the downs. I've had access to a network of business academics and advisors at the forefront of their game, from marketing strategy to legal advice, and the university has provided invaluable expertise across a variety of fields.

Jack Preston, Yaantu

brilliant example

National Association of College and University Entrepreneurs

Over the last six years the National Association of College and University Entrepreneurs (NACUE) has engaged over 180,000 students in enterprising and entrepreneurial activities, supported a network of over 260 enterprise societies, and seen over 18,000 people attend its events.

Its community alone has generated over 1,600 businesses, including Amaliah, a 'modest fashion' website for modern Muslim women. Nafisa Bakkar from University College London launched the business in 2015 after support from NACUE and helped turn her dream into reality.

It was after attending the NACUE Student Enterprise Conference and meeting other student and graduate entrepreneurs that she quit her job and dedicated herself full time to the business.

Attending NACUE's conference was a real turning point for Nafisa. 'Going to SEC and being surrounded by like-minded and ambitious individuals from all backgrounds, contexts and degrees made me realise that I too could actually do it', says Nafisa. She has now been named as one the UK's top start-ups by the British Council and has been accepted into the Ignite accelerator programme.

Johnny Luk, CEO, National Association of
Colleges and University Entrepreneurs

It's not all about money. Increasingly, students are driven by developing ideas for a common good – to make a difference to a community. Even larger corporations have developed a commitment to sustainability by investing in both social and environmental projects. The main difference when developing a social enterprise is that all of the profits are ploughed back into the business.

There are several examples of successful social enterprises. Here are three: The Big Issue, Eden Project and Divine Chocolate. Social enterprise enables students to develop a small business idea and demonstrate how they resonate with the corporate values of the organisations which they may work for in the future. Integrity and an ability to demonstrate ethical attributes will provide students with an ability to stand out in society, which now places much more emphasis on these characteristics.

Business challenges

Business challenges present another avenue for exploring enterprise at university. Many universities run replica *Dragon's Den* competitions or business challenges, which allow students to explore their entrepreneurial skills. There are many schemes in operation, so do your research, see what's already running at your university or scout out businesses that offer schemes for you to get involved. Challenges also give you an opportunity to increase your business awareness and engage with numerous organisations. Here are a few examples:

- L'Oreal Brainstorm Competition: http://www.brandstorm.loreal.com/

- Adecco Way to Work, CEO for the month: https://www.adeccowaytowork.com/

- CIMA Global Business Challenge: www.cimaglobal.com/Events-and-cpd-courses/globalbusinesschallenge/

---

brilliant example

MyKindaFuture Online challenges

An online challenge is an innovative way for companies to engage with students from schools, colleges or universities. It requires minimal internal resource from the employer but provides a means of effective engagement with young people across different age groups. Students are more engaged and receptive to business messages when responding to a challenge, as it allows them to get under the skin of a business and brand and form a more meaningful connection.

The Universities Business Challenge (UBC) is the UK's longest established and most recognised simulation-based competitive challenge for undergraduates designed to develop employability, enterprise skills and entrepreneurship. Supported by leading universities and IBM, a leading

▷

graduate employer, more than 25,000 students have benefitted from participating in the UBC Worldwide over the past 18 years.

Enterprise and entrepreneurship skills are incredibly attractive to graduate employers and recruiters, so all three rounds of the UBC are designed to develop these skills in a team-based competitive challenge.

Undergraduate students are given the opportunity to work as a board of directors in realistic, simulated companies, making all the critical business decisions that affect performance. The UBC simulations are varied and challenging, and range from manufacturing to service businesses and social enterprises to offer a rounded learning experience.

The UBC complements classroom learning and provides a learning-by-doing experience which embeds taught theory. Not only for business studies students, it is a true learning experience for all those who enter, no matter what their study discipline. It will help students to improve their understanding of how businesses work, develop their decision-making skills, their team-working abilities and increase their knowledge in key business areas such as marketing, finance, strategy, production, pricing and HR.

In addition to business and management studies, students from other faculties such as information technology, engineering, economics, accounting, law and a wide range of arts and science faculties have gained a new understanding of the business world and at the same time have developed their employability and enterprise skills.

Deborah Cardwell, Managing Director, UBC Worldwide

Sport

Whether you play basketball, netball, tennis, hockey or football you are developing employability skills. Sport represents an opportunity for students to actively demonstrate their employability skills. Being a team captain, being the spokesperson for the team or motivating team members are valuable skills.

At university, students are encouraged to get involved in sport, as it provides opportunities to travel, meet students from other universities and gain recognition for success, within the university, and also nationally and internationally. British Universities & Colleges Sport provides numerous opportunities for students to play a sport both nationally and internationally. The national leagues and championships, including the World University and European Union Championships, are the perfect addition to your experience at university.

---

brilliant example

The role of volunteer student football activator

While at university I took on the role of volunteer student football activator, supported by the Football Association (FA) and my university. It required me to plan, organise, market and deliver football activities that engaged other students within the university, specifically those not already playing football. Through the role I was able to develop skills that have helped massively in getting a job and I am now working successfully as a paramedic.

In a clinical setting, effective communication and leadership skills are invaluable in often difficult and pressurised situations. Through my role as an activator, I had the opportunity to develop these skills within my relationships and engagement with players, referees and volunteers. I was able to enhance and develop my leadership skills when delivering informal 'Just Play' sessions which week on week attracted over 100 participants.

Challenges included catering to so many different abilities and expectations while delivering as much contact time as possible to all interested players. Almost without knowing, I developed the ability to manage a crisis related to inadequate facilities and players' patience. Developing resilience and problem-solving skills has stood me in good stead for when things don't always go to plan as a paramedic.

The activator role has definitely given me the skills that have supported my employment and career so far as a paramedic. Without the leadership, communication, problem-solving and resilience developed through volunteering in sport I would be much less effective within my role.

Josh, university football activator (volunteer) and now a paramedic

Course representatives

You are already on a course, so why not be the course rep? The name may vary but essentially the role involves you being the voice of students on the course at academic course management meetings. Students are encouraged to seek the views and opinions of their fellow students and let the course team know the issues students are facing.

The role can be challenging, especially if there are significant issues, but it provides a platform to develop management skills, such as gathering and preparing information before the meeting, informing students of your role and willingness to represent them, the ability to communicate with senior course management and defend students' needs.

The skills developed in being a course representative highlight your ability to network, listen, gather opinions and communicate at various levels.

brilliant example

Mechanical engineering course representative

I was excited to be elected course representative. There were five candidates and only two places. I prepared a speech, which outlined my interpretation of the role, and I received the most votes. I assured students of their anonymity and gave them plenty of time to provide me with their views and opinions prior to meetings. I would also make announcements at the end of lectures advising students of the forthcoming course boards and my availability.

Now, as a team leader, I adopt the same approach. I give my team opportunities to discuss concerns about senior management decisions and in turn I am the collective voice of my team.

Mechanical engineering graduate

Part-time work

Whether you are serving at a checkout, stacking shelves or waiting tables, you are developing your employability skills. Your experience may not be directly related to your future, but performing well in your role will add value to your CV. Being punctual, your length of service and developing customer service skills are all transferable to your career goals.

Employers need reliable employees who value their customers and take pride in their work. References are requested regardless of the industry sector you choose, so a glowing reference from your previous employer will always be welcomed by a future employer.

If you are going to work part time, be the best that you can be. If there are opportunities to be the employee of the month, be a team leader or take on extra responsibility, then seize these opportunities. To show advancement in your part-time job is a demonstration of your commitment, dedication and ability to excel.

---

brilliant example

From part-time to full-time work

My journey with M&S began when I decided to apply for a Saturday job alongside starting in the sixth form. I had always taken an interest in retail as I saw beyond what the everyday customer eventually views on the shelf and the experience they receive when they purchase that item.

I wanted to have an influence on the process behind the product and service that led me to seek out additional responsibility in my role. I learnt about the core processes and key parts to successful retailing and this was recognised by my line manager at the time, who advised me of the opportunities for progression internally. After following the same

▶

application process as an external candidate I was successful in gaining a place on the M&S placement programme.

I spent a year on a placement as part of my degree, which gave me invaluable experience in retail management across areas where I would have previously felt nervous and lacking in confidence, such as people management, communication and sales. The end-result was a graduate role at head office where, after completing the graduate scheme, I still work.

Joey Hosier, Customer Experience Manager,

Marks and Spencer plc

Becoming a global graduate

Increasingly, organisations operate globally and whether you physically travel overseas or are a part of an international virtual team, students will be expected to have a degree of cultural sensitivity.

One way to develop additional employability skills is to undertake an international internship. Not only does this make for interesting reading on your application forms, but also demonstrates a wide range of skills. For example, in some cases it develops resilience, but overall it shows a willingness to seize an opportunity and venture into the unknown. Graduates, who have opted to travel overseas, are often able to demonstrate a wider range of employability skills and a better appreciation of cultural differences.

brilliant example

Benefits of an international internship

We live in a world full of opportunity, choice and potential. And yet, the job market today is the most competitive it has ever been and youth unemployment is a large national concern.

Companies are able to select from a vast pool of qualified candidates. Unique experiences and skills are what set people apart from the general pool of applicants. And employers keep an eye out for graduates who are globally aware and have dynamic talent with leadership potential.

Pave, a company providing students and graduates with internships in India, believes that internships have the power to provide young career professionals with life-changing experiences that help them grow. Pave provides its interns with a once-in-a-lifetime, cross-cultural experience that gives young adults the opportunity to develop personally, gain professional skills in a challenging work environment and secure international experience that is imperative to success in the job market.

James Thomas and Apoorva Chaudry,
Managing Directors, Pave

Preparing for an international internship

Travelling overseas is a great opportunity, but students need to prepare for it. Some countries will require visas, vaccinations and possibly work permits. It is therefore necessary to do your research. There are many sources of information, such as the company organising the international internship or the Foreign and Common Wealth Office (FCO), that can provide a checklist to ensure there are no issues when you travel. Having adequate travel insurance is a must in the event of an incident, so that you are able access the support you need without question. Do not save on travel insurance as it will cost you in the long run if you fall ill on your trip.

brilliant tip

Top tips for choosing an international internship

● Always look for funding available from your university, national or regional government bodies or destination-specific foundations or scholarships.

- Ask for an interview with the company, preferably over a video call, to discuss the exact details of the internship and projects you'll be working on.

- Do some due diligence on the company you'll be interning with, by checking sites such as GoOverseas.com, RateMyPlacement.com, TheStudentRoom.co.uk and Glassdoor.com.

- Ask for references from students who have done an internship at the company in the past.

- Don't rule out small and medium-sized companies (SMEs) over well-known brands, as sometimes they offer more insight and the application process can be less competitive.

- Don't pay a deposit to a third-party provider of internships overseas without knowing exactly what it can help you with and which company you'll be working with.

Top tips for keeping safe abroad

- Check the FCO website for any travel advice for high-risk areas.

- Check with your GP that you have the relevant vaccinations for the trip.

- Check your level of health and travel insurance cover carefully, in particular excess levels, adequate medical cover including repatriation and limits on valuable items covered.

- Make two emergency documents, keeping one with you and one somewhere safe such as at your accommodation. The documents should include copies of your passport, a list of emergency contact numbers and your insurance policy details.

- Don't carry too much cash at any one time or leave valuable items on show in public places, especially mobile phones.

Jamie Bettles, Managing Director, Intern China Ltd

Developing additional skills

Learning, knowledge and technology are constantly moving, so while at university it is always a good idea to do a review. Are there any short courses that could be beneficial to your future career or complement your degree? A language course, a marketing course or a course in business planning? It does not have to be academic – it could be to further develop an interest or hobby.

In recent years there has been an explosion of online and short courses. There are different opportunities to develop additional skills: distance learning, blended learning or face to face. There are many providers that offer the opportunity to undertake short courses in a plethora of subjects, which will ultimately be of benefit to you upon graduation. Examples of providers include:

- General Assembly: https://generalassemb.ly
- Lynda.com: www.lynda.com
- Udemy.com: www.udemy.com

---

brilliant examples

Courses with General Assembly

University can be an exciting and vitally important time in anyone's personal, emotional and intellectual development. It's an important time to learn many things including learning how to learn. Many students graduate without a strong grasp of the day-to-day skills and proficiencies they will need to enter the workforce.

At General Assembly we are confronting this skills gap by providing best-in-class instruction and access to a global community of alumni and hiring partners to help students pursue the work they love. Our instructors are expert practitioners in their field and our courses supplement a degree by focusing on the most relevant and in-demand skills across data, design, business and technology.

Through teaching students the critical tools and methods they need to succeed in a variety of careers, we will help apply the theory learned in university and convert this knowledge into hard skills that employers are looking for such as coding, UX design, data analysis, digital marketing and more. Plus, you'll walk away with projects, portfolios and prototypes that help showcase skills and abilities to potential employers.

Julien Deslangles-Blanch, Regional Director, General Assembly London

Have you heard about HEAR?

The High Education Achievement Report (HEAR) is a single electronic record of students' achievements and accomplishments through their degree. Upon leaving university students not only receive a degree certificate, but also an electronic record of all academic and extracurricular achievements.

The purpose of the HEAR is to provide a comprehensive account of a student's experience at university to help employers gain a more holistic picture of a student's accomplishments, and enable students to maintain an accurate account of their achievements. The standardisation of the report also enables employers to compare candidates based on their experiences at university.

The HEAR has the following sections:

- Introductory text outlining the context
- Section 1: Student's personal details
- Section 2: Name of the qualification
- Section 3: Level of the qualification
- Section 4: Details of content and results gained
- Section 5: Details of the function of the qualification
- Section 6: Additional information including awards and prizes
- Section 7: Formal authentication

- Section 8: Weblink reference to a description of the National Higher Education system to which the qualification and higher education institution belongs.

Currently, 90 universities and colleges are implementing or planning to implement the HEAR. This includes 32 institutions that have already issued 427,000 HEARs to students – and this number is increasing annually.

Not just a degree

Don't be fooled: your grades do matter. Level 4 students often state this in their first year at university. Often the grades from your first year do not count towards your final degree classification. If you intend on applying for a summer internship, you may need to submit your transcript of your grades.

Graduating with the best class of degree you can is paramount. Missing assignments or skipping classes will make it harder for you to graduate with a Brilliant degree. Tom Peters in his book *In Search of Excellence* (Peters, 2004) writes that no one is searching for mediocrity.

Look at it from an employer's perspective: if you had a vacancy, wouldn't you want the best student in the class? Therefore monitor your grades and aim for a first-class degree. Often students do not understand how their degree is graded. Make sure you know what percentage of your marks each year counts towards your final degree classification and set goals for each year of study, like the one below.

Degree classification	Year one	Year two	Year three
% of marks towards final degree classification of your degree	e.g. 0%, must pass all first-year units	e.g. 20% of total marks	e.g. 80% of final marks

brilliant example

Graduating with a 2:2

I graduated with a 2:2 and it was a struggle to secure my first graduate position. When I attended graduate recruitment fairs companies only wanted people with 2:1s or above. It was a real blow to be rejected by so many companies. Luckily I had more to offer having completed two years of volunteering while at university and was also very active in sports. It took 40 applications, 35 rejections, ten interviews and nine months of stress to gain my first graduate position.

A business graduate

The same applies for the assessment of each of your units. How many units should you complete in each academic year and how are they assessed? To be successful you must know the 'rules of the game'. Complete the table below for your year of study, so you are clear about how each unit will be assessed.

Unit or module	Assessment criteria
Unit 1	
Unit 2	
Unit 3	
Unit 4	
Unit 5	
Unit 6	

brilliant Question

Why should students get involved in extracurricular activities?
To give you an opportunity to experience the world of work and to develop additional skills. It's great if you can look to secure a short-term

placement or internship which puts you into an organisation. However, employability can still be developed through involvement with activities on campus or through projects so think laterally about what suits you best and then think about how you best position and sell those experiences in the applications that you make.

Helen Alkin, Head of Future Talent Recruitment,

Marks and Spencer plc

brilliant recap

- If 72% of students are graduating with a 2:1 or a first, you cannot rely on your degree to make you stand out. So your extracurricular activities and work experience will be the focus of most employers.

- A degree allows you to enter the arena, but it is your involvement in developing relevant employability skills that will differentiate you from the competition and help secure a graduate position.

- Work experience is vital in order to be successful upon graduation.

- There is a definitive relationship between universities and the development of employability skills, but ultimately it is your responsibility.

- The skills developed as a result of completing assessments are directly transferable to the work environment.

- Get involved – don't let opportunities pass you by.

- Don't use lack of time as an excuse – make time as it's your future.

- Is there a society that interests you or do you want to start your own society? Take the time to investigate.

- Volunteering adds value to you and the organisations. Even if it's just an hour a week or a one-day team challenge, find out what you can offer.

- Whether you want to start your own business or just develop enterprise skills, there are many opportunities to explore at university.

- Review your role as team player, captain or coach and identify how this translates into the world of work.

- Be your course representative – develop managerial skills while studying for your degree.

- Part-time work can present opportunities to develop your employability but also present career opportunities upon graduation. Make sure you perform to the best of your ability. Don't wait for a sign labelled 'opportunity'.

- Make sure you know how your degree classification is determined and how each of your units is assessed. How can you succeed if you don't know how you are being measured?

CHAPTER 4

The job market

Developing your I Brand is not
an option: it's a prerequisite for
success!

on't underestimate the challenge of finding a graduate position. The graduate market is highly competitive and the number of graduates in the marketplace far outstrips the number of jobs available. The key fact to remember is there are opportunities and every year companies recruit to their graduate schemes. You just need to be ready to compete.

One aspect of your preparation is understanding your industry sector. What are the recruiters in your sector looking for? What issues are they facing with current applications from graduates? What areas of the sector do they see in contraction or expansion? Use this information to ensure that you are developing the right skills. How, though, do you access this information?

What is a graduate scheme?

The majority of top employers offer a graduate training scheme. This is an opportunity for companies to recruit the best graduate talent into their organisations. Graduates are recruited from a wide range of degree disciplines into a wide range of roles. The purpose of graduate training schemes is to offer students the opportunity to experience various roles within an organisation before deciding upon a specialism.

Companies invest in the training and development of their graduate talent, their leaders of tomorrow. As a result, the training presents a range of opportunities and exposure to various departments and individuals, but requires dedication and hard work from graduates. In turn, graduates are rewarded with a competitive salary, career opportunities and a targeted training and development programme.

In order to be successful in gaining a place on a graduate scheme, students need to start their search at least a year before graduation to ensure they are aware of company deadlines and recruitment procedures. A typical recruitment process will include:

- the completion of an online application form
- a telephone interview
- psychometric testing
- invitation to an assessment centre, including a face-to-face interview.

brilliant tip

Getting the basics right

Every year a significant number of graduate vacancies go unfilled, despite employers receiving over 60 applications per vacancy. Employers search for the mix of knowledge, skills and attributes that will make their organisations perform effectively. Getting the right job may seem a daunting task fraught with uncertainty. But get the basics right and it could be more straightforward than you think.

- **Know thyself.** Socrates may not have realised it but he was disseminating careers advice 2,400 years ago. Reflect on what tasks you are good at, enjoy and can do well even when tired. Then look for an area of work that will let you deploy your talents.

- **Be passionate.** If you enjoy reading the *Financial Times* at the weekend you will probably enjoy a business career. If the sight of blood doesn't make you faint maybe you should be a medic. To be successful you need to work hard and you will only work hard at a thing over a long period of time if you are passionate about it.

- **Understand that a group assignment is not teamwork.** Every student completes a group project at some point in their academic career. When did you get something done with and through others when you weren't told to? This is teamwork.

- **Admit mistakes.** The candidate who has not made a mistake is either lying or hasn't pushed him or herself. It's ok to make mistakes as long as you learn from them and don't repeat them.

- **Try on the shoes of your interviewer.** Recruiters want to hire people. Rejecting a candidate is a negative outcome and, in essence, is wasted time. Think about it. What is your prospective employer looking for? What will make them invest time and resources in hiring you? Would you hire yourself?

Be the candidate that gets the offer call – someone will.

Stephen Isherwood, Chief Executive,
Association of Graduate Recruiters

Overview of the graduate market

Despite the continued growth in the graduate market since the recession in 2007, the graduate market still remains increasingly competitive. Not only are you competing with current graduates but also with graduates who have not found positions in previous years. The Destination of Leavers in Higher Education Report (DLHE, 2015) stated that in 2013/14 there were 424,375 UK and EU leavers (UK 398,105 and EU 2,270). This represents almost a 50% increase in the number of leavers compared to a decade ago. In 2015 the number of graduate vacancies was the highest since the recession in 2007 with a total of 22,300 vacancies. (High Fliers Research, 2016)

Despite this increase, the Association of Graduate Recruiters also noted that there has been a steady decline in the number of applications received per graduate vacancy. In 2012/13 there were 85 applications per vacancy and this number has decreased every year with only 69 application in 2013/14 compared with 65 in 2014/15. (AGR, 2016, p. 32)

This is good news for students graduating, but when the actual number of applications received is considered it is a staggering 4,522 applications per graduate scheme. The importance of being able to communicate your skills and attributes becomes even more important in order to stand out. As stated previously, there are an increasing amount of graduates (72%) graduating with a 2:1 or a first, which increases the importance of engaging in extracurricular activities to ensure your application has a clear unique selling point.

The graduate market is improving, with a forecast increase in 2014 of 8%, which High Fliers Research states is the 'largest annual rise for four years'. The graduates of 2016 could expect a further 7.5% rise in 2015. The competition is still as fierce as ever, but you always have to keep in mind that there are positions available and you only need one company and one job. You will be rejected on several occasions, but you need to keep going until you find a company that can see the brilliance in you.

---

brilliant example

Graduate employment

When the global recession took hold in 2008, graduate employment was one of the first parts of the UK economy to be hit. In little more than 18 months, organisations featured in *The Times Top 100 Graduate Employers* cut their graduate vacancies by almost a quarter, leaving tens of thousands of university-leavers either unemployed or in jobs that didn't require them to have a degree.

It has been a long slow recovery since, but by the summer of 2015, graduate recruitment at the country's top employers finally returned to pre-recession levels and several of the UK's most sought-after organisations were reporting a record number of entry-level vacancies.

The outlook for 2016 seems even more upbeat with the number of jobs on offer for new graduates expected to increase by a further 8% (see figure below).

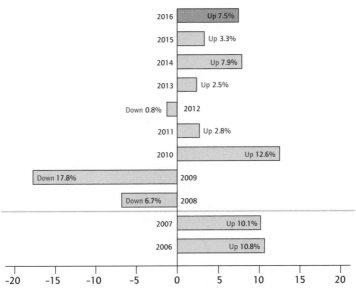

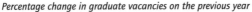

Percentage change in graduate vacancies on the previous year

Source: The Graduate Marker 2016, © High Fliers Research Limited 2016

Graduate pay is also increasing. After four consecutive years when starting salaries were frozen, the median package for new graduates with one of the UK's leading employers in 2016 is expected to be £30,000, with even more generous salaries on offer from the top City investment banks (an average of £47,000), law firms (£41,000) and banking and finance firms (£36,000). In the table below is a list of graduate salaries in 2016 by industry or business sector.

	Median graduate starting salaries for 2016
Accounting and professional services	£30,300
Armed Forces	£30,000
Banking and Finance	£36,000
Consulting	£31,500
Consumer Goods	£29,000
Engineering and Industrial	£26,000
Investment banking	£47,000
IT & Telecommunications	£30,000
Law	£41,000
Media	£27,000
Oil and Energy	£32,500
Public sector	£21,000
Retailing	£26,000

Source: The Graduate Marker 2016, © High Fliers Research Limited 2016

Despite this upbeat picture, there remains a word of warning. The number of new graduates leaving university from full-time undergraduate degree courses in the summer of 2016 is expected to top 400,000 for the first time – nearly double the number who graduated from UK universities 20 years ago. And yet there are unlikely to be more than 200,000 graduate-level vacancies available across all parts of the UK employment market.

This means inevitably that even in a comparatively buoyant job market, many of those graduating from the 'Class of 2016' – almost all of whom have invested up to £9,000 per year on tuition fees – will still face tough competition to land their first graduate job.

Martin Birchall, Editor, *The Times Top 100 Graduate Employers* and Managing Director, High Fliers Research

The range of graduate vacancies

The Destination of Higher Education Leavers Report 2015 stated that 68% of the 2013/14 first full-time degree leavers, whose destinations were known, found full-time employment classified as professional.

Although the High Fliers Research report 2016 states that graduate vacancies are at an all time high since the recession, with a further increase due in 2016, the number of vacancies is still not representative of the number of students graduating. Another concern is the fact that in 2015 alone 1,000 graduate vacancies among the top 100 employers were left unfilled. This is an alarming figure as it only represents those companies covered in the survey. You begin to question how many graduate vacancies were left unfilled if we were to consider all of the graduate employers.

In 2016 the accounting and professional services firms, public sector employees, engineering and industrial firms and investments banks will represent 70% of the graduate vacancies. Despite the growth in the number of vacancies, graduates should note that 32% of these vacancies will be filled by those who have already engaged with the company either through work experience, internship or placement. (High Fliers Research, 2016)

It is therefore in students' interest to research carefully companies where they wish to undertake work experience, internships or placements.

The location of 80% of graduate vacancies will be in London, with the second highest region being the south east of England, followed by the south west and north west. Despite companies trying to highlight opportunities in other regions of the country, London still dominates the graduate sector for vacancies.

The other interesting factor about graduate vacancies is the range functions, which are more likely to generate graduate vacancies. IT graduate vacancies top the table at 55%, which is reflective of the digital and technological age that organisations operate within. Finance and human resources are in second and third place with 51% and 39% respectively.

The fact that IT tops the table with the number of graduate vacancies demonstrates that IT skills are wanted at more than just IT companies. It proliferates many sectors and plays an important role within the accounting, public sector, banking and engineering sector.

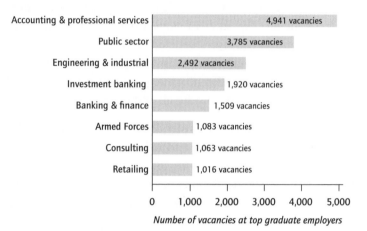

Number of vacancies at top graduate employers

Source: The Graduate Marker 2016, © High Fliers Research Limited 2016

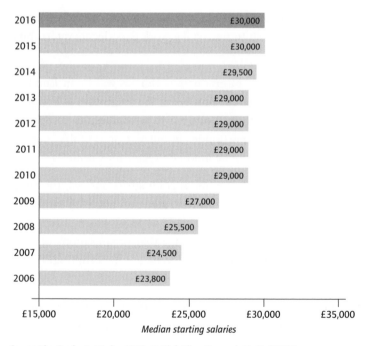

Median starting salaries

Source: The Graduate Marker 2016, © High Fliers Research Limited 2016

Work experience

The vacancies in relation to placements and internships emphasise the level of importance placed by employers on students gaining work experience. Employers recognise their role in making these opportunities available, in order to develop students' employability skills.

Some 59% of the UK's top 100 graduate employers offered 6- to 12-month industrial placements. Seventy-six per cent of UK's top 100 graduate employers provide paid internships or vacation placements for penultimate year undergraduates.

By engaging with students at this early stage in their studies, employers are able to identify suitable candidates for their graduate schemes. Internships and placements enable organisations to build relationships with promising students. This is further illustrated in the data as a third of all graduate roles are filled by graduates who have already worked for the employer during their degree.

Sixteen per cent of the UK's top employers in 2016 have more than 250 work experience places. This further emphasises the desire of employers to engage with undergraduates, but also illustrates their willingness to provide opportunities for students to gain experience in the marketplace. Graduates with no work experience will find it hard to compete as companies want students to be able to provide practical demonstrations of their employability skills.

The table below lists the number of paid work experience places by industry or business sector.

Industry/sector	Total work experience places available in 2016
Accounting and professional services	2,337
Banking and finance	1,484
Consulting	210
Consumer goods	385

(continued)

Industry/sector	Total work experience places available in 2016
Engineering and industrial	1,675
Investment banking	2,615
IT and telecommunications	520
Law	1,030
Oil and energy	322
Public sector	2,339
Retailing	339

Source: The Graduate Market in 2016, High Fliers Research

It is important to emphasise the need for work experience. Undertaking an internship or placement is a chance for the company to trial your 'product' and, if the company is impressed, you can receive preference for their graduate schemes. It is therefore essential to gain work experience relevant to a sector of interest.

Diversity and graduate recruitment

Organisations monitor diversity data to ensure that they are receiving applications from a range of candidates and can introduce measures where necessary to increase the diversity of applications and recruits from under-represented groups.

The Association of Graduate Recruiters (AGR) found in its 2015 annual survey that in 2013/14 there was a significant disparity between females hired: 41.6% compared to 58.7% who graduated in the same period. This is not the same when compared to data related to Black, Asian and minority ethnic hires. The disparity between actual hires 15.6% and the number of undergraduates at 18.6% was very minimal.

The other dimension of diversity employers measured was socioeconomic background. Ninety-five per cent gauged socioeconomic background by capturing data on whether graduates were the first in their family to attend university. Other indicators included the attendance at state or private schooling (82.5%) and whether the graduate had claimed free school meals (62.5%).

Nearly 90% of graduate recruiters monitored levels of diversity with almost 80% having an active strategy to monitor and improve the levels of diversity in their graduate hires. It was found that 62.8% of employers focused their efforts on increasing the levels of diversity in relation to gender, compared to 43.9% that actively sought to increase the ethnic diversity of their staff.

Challenges facing graduate recruiters

To address the continued amount of graduate hires who reneged on graduate vacancies, which on average was 8.2% in 2015, employers made offers to 111 applicants for every 100 positions. The number of graduate hires who reneged once having accepted the position, increased with accounting and professional services to 12.9% and banking and financial services to 12.8%. But it is the engineering and industrial companies that offer the highest with 118.3% of offers for every 100 graduate positions, and 115% for the public sector. This suggests an underlying problem to attract talent or a shortage of candidates.

Industry or sector

Understanding your industry or sector is paramount. To be successful you need to be aware of the skills needed to compete in your chosen field. There are many ways to develop industry-specific knowledge. Joining a professional body can provide you with regular updates, e-bulletins and networking opportunities with professionals from your chosen industry. The careers service will have specific information on the sector and information on the various roles found within the industry.

Your degree will also provide you with a range of industry-specific links from websites to journals to industry speakers. Using the alumni is another avenue to not only find out about the industry but also possible opportunities for work experience in their organisation.

Your degree

Employability is embedded in the curriculum and your lectures and assessments will present current trends in your industry. Your assignments will include research into changes in the industry, company-specific case studies and future developments impacting the development of the sector. As a result, your course is one of the first sources of information about the industry.

Reading material will be targeted and provide an insight into industry trends, industry-sector journals and magazines and relevant websites. Lecturers will often invite industry professionals to deliver lectures on challenges facing the industry and changes in the macro-environment impacting the organisation.

Joining a professional body

All industries have a professional body or network which can provide an insight into the industry. Becoming a member is not as expensive as you may think (student membership can range from £20 to £40). Below is a sample of professional bodies and their membership fees.

Institution of Civil Engineers (www.ice.org.uk)

Annual student membership: free

Benefits of membership:

- free access to the online version of *Civil Engineering*
- free access to the online version of *New Civil Engineer*
- question and answer support service
- access to the ICE library

- bi-monthly e-newsletter
- free access to ICE virtual library
- eligible for ICE awards and prizes
- eligibility to join the students and graduate network.

The Writers' Guild (www.writersguild.org.uk)

Annual student membership: £20

Benefits of membership:

- support and advice
- weekly e-bulletin
- *UK Writer* magazine (quarterly)
- events featuring established writers and industry specialists
- discounts.

Do some research to find your professional body as it will keep your industry information and links with industry professionals current.

---

brilliant example

British Computer Society membership

I felt so prepared when I started to look for graduate positions. As a member of the British Computer Society I had kept up to date with the industry news and also attended a number of talks by industry professionals. As a result, I had an understanding of the trends and their impact on the current climate. When I went for interviews I could speak quite confidently about the sector and had even formed my own opinions as to forthcoming changes. Interviewers were very impressed with my industry knowledge.

An information technology graduate

Careers service

Don't forget to use the wealth of experience available in your careers service. The advisors will have links with employers and can advise you on the expectations of graduate recruiters. There are also degree-specific graduate industry magazines that can provide you with additional information. The careers service will also organise a number of graduate and placement fairs, presenting opportunities for you to speak directly with employers.

Alumni network

You are not the first to graduate from your course, so learn from the experiences of others. Use the alumni to field questions about expectations in the graduate market. How hard was it to find a job? What was the interview process? How many jobs did you apply for and when? Alumni are a valuable source of information so either contact your alumni office or speak to lecturers about asking students from previous years to give a talk to the current cohort.

---

brilliant example

The alumni network

I owe my first graduate position to an alumnus of my university. He came to talk to our class about his journey after graduation. We were talking after the event and I asked him if we could go for a coffee one day. He became my sounding board. I would ask him to review my CV or for his view on career pathways. When I graduated, he convinced his manager to give me a three-month temporary contract. At the end of that period I was made permanent. Finding out about the industry from someone who graduated from your course is priceless.

A business graduate

Company annual reports and websites

Annual reports and websites display current information about both the industry and the company. This is displayed in many formats including downloadable reports or video content. It's a valuable online resource and can provide insight into both the company and the sector. Companies need to attract the brightest and the best, so it is in their interest to provide as much information as possible to attract the right candidates.

Review the website of the company you would like to work for. How informative is its website about the company or about the industry? Can you register for any e-bulletins or newsletters?

brilliant recap

- A graduate scheme is an opportunity for companies to recruit the best graduate talent.

- Graduates are recruited from a wide range of degree disciplines into a wide range of roles.

- In 2016 graduate vacancies have risen to pre-recession levels.

- The majority of industries or business sectors are experiencing a growth in their recruitment targets, with public sector, banking and finance employers and engineering and industrial companies experiencing a significant increase.

- The number of graduate positions available in IT and telecommunications has seen an increase in 219% from 2006 to 2016. (High Fliers Research, 2016)

- More than 80% of graduate recruiters offered graduate vacancies in London, followed by 51% in the south east. (High Fliers Research, 2016)

- £30,000 was the average salary with investment banking topping the table at £47,000.

- Companies use internships and placements to trial your 'product' and, if impressed, will aim to offer you a place on their graduate scheme.

- Knowledge is power so make sure you research your industry and leading competitors. Be aware of developing industry challenges and trends.

- Research the professional body associated with your degree and find out what hints and tips they offer to students.

- Use all the resources available to you, such as the university careers service or alumni network.

- Company websites will provide you with an insight into the company and the industry.

- Learn from the experiences of previous graduates on your course. They will be able to give you their experience of the industry and advice on finding a job in it.

CHAPTER 5

Social media, jobs and you

Are you LinkedIn? If graduate recruiters saw your Facebook profile would they withdraw their job offer?

Eighty-nine per cent of the *The Times'* top 100 graduate employers use social media to promote graduate opportunities (High Flier Research, 2016). With 1.09 billion Facebook users and 310 million daily Twitter users and an average of 400 million LinkedIn users (Source Statista), it's a cost-effective choice for employers to access their target market through social media for less than the traditional methods of advertising.

Despite social media being such a viable platform, only 3% of graduates in 2013/14 found their graduate position using social media (according to the Destination of Leavers from Higher Education Survey). Social media has become a useful tool to not only finding employment, but also to research companies and engage with them prior to working for the organisation. You can use social media to create your personal brand and market yourself to companies, but it also allow companies to find you.

LinkedIn

Professionals from all sectors have profiles on LinkedIn, making it the perfect medium to network. Networking opportunities are not limited to identifying individuals within your field, but also extend to joining professional networks and alumni groups. The opportunities for networking possibilities are endless and students cannot afford to not engage with this platform.

brilliant action

Use LinkedIn to find a graduate job

There are lots of graduate jobs on LinkedIn. If you are interested in specific employers, search for them using the search bar at the top of the page to access a company page. Follow the companies you are interested in to receive news, market insights, culture insights and jobs in your LinkedIn newsfeed on your home page.

Many companies have a careers page – look for the tab or link on the company page. This will give you more information about different careers at that company, and also direct you to a list of all the current live jobs. When looking at the live jobs, use the filters on the left-hand side to drill down to the jobs that are right for you – filter by location, by keyword (in the advanced section), and also use the experience filter to select entry-level jobs.

You don't have to get to jobs via a company page as you can use the top navigation link 'Jobs' to get to the Jobs main page. There you can customise your preferences (on location, industry, etc.) to inform LinkedIn of the type of jobs you want to see. It will use these data, together with information (keywords) in your profile, to provide job recommendations to you.

The more complete and accurate your profile, the better the recommendations are going to be. From the Jobs main page you can search on keywords for jobs, not exclusive to a company, and then use the filters to zoom into the right sort of jobs for you.

When you look at a job, LinkedIn will also give you some useful additional information, such as 'People also viewed' and 'Similar jobs'. It is helping you out by taking a job that is in the right area and showing you other jobs that could well match what you are looking for. This expands your search in ways you may not have thought of and to companies you might not have heard of.

Before applying for a job, also look at whether you know anyone at the company. LinkedIn will tell you if you have any connections there who you might ask for some useful insights about working there. Or you might have a second degree connection – you know someone who knows someone else at that company – and maybe you could get an introduction.

Or check if there are alumni from your university who now work at that company. You can do this by going to your university's page on LinkedIn, or www.linkedin.com/alumni. Use the filters to select the company and other information such as location and/or industry. LinkedIn will show you graduate alumni who now work there – and one of them might be able to give you some help.

Charles Hardy, Higher Education Leader, LinkedIn

A LinkedIn profile

But how do you make yourself stand out when there are so many users on the platform? How will an employer find me?

brilliant tip

How to create your LinkedIn profile

First impressions are very important so start with your photo. You need to have one, as you are more likely to attract attention with one, but it needs to be the right photo.

- It must be professional – how you would like to be perceived in a work environment.
- It should be a head and shoulders shot of decent quality, showing your eyes.
- You should be smiling – you want people to want to work with you.
- Think of where you want to work. If it's in accountancy, what do people wear in their photos? Or if it's in web development, you might be better looking casual, even wearing a T-shirt.

▶

- Do not use an image, cartoon, pet, holiday snap or party photo.
- Do not be far away or hidden in some way.

Personalise your headline. This is one of the first things a person sees when they view your profile (even before then in Search results), so it's your first chance to make a deeper impression. It defaults to your latest job title but you can customise it at any time. Saying 'Student' won't make you stand out to a recruiter so insert concisely what you have done, what you are doing and (most importantly) what you want to do in the future. For example: Currently studying Economics | Graduate in 2017 | Interested in a career in digital communications and social media integration

Understand the importance of your keywords. LinkedIn matches jobs to you based on your profile content and on keywords in your profile. Employers search on LinkedIn for people they want to hire using keywords. So draw up four or five keywords by asking yourself: Who do you want to be found by? What do you want to be found for? If you were them, what would you search for?

Include your keywords in your headline, your summary and your skills – these are all 'super-powered keyword' sections.

Use the summary to promote your potential. This is your 'Elevator Pitch', a concise pitch on who you are and what you want to do, and why you would be great. Having an Elevator Pitch is great for interviews and careers fairs, not just on LinkedIn. You should be able to say it in around 30 seconds, and it should have a little of what you have done such as qualifications and experience, but really be focused on the future and what you want to do, and what interests you. Use the first person (I am. . .).

Employers are not hiring graduates based on your extensive work experience, but for your potential to come in and help their business develop and succeed in the future. They are looking for potential, enthusiasm, interest, passion and drive.

So it is important that you demonstrate this in your profile (and at an interview) – add links to a blog or attach a presentation from a project or research, follow relevant companies or join relevant groups.

Share useful and interesting content related to the career direction you are looking at.

All these things will shine in your profile and give employers confidence you are the right person for them.

Complete the work experience section with jobs you have done, including internships and placements, and even part-time summer jobs as they add value to your profile, showing you have been employed, are responsible and have worked in a team. Be concise, use bullet points, use power words, such as 'managed', 'responsible for', 'delivered' and 'led'.

Complete the education section – make sure you add your university (select from the dropdown list and check the logo is added to your profile). Include details about your course, and even add in white papers as attachments if relevant for your career direction.

There are lots of sections you can complete on your LinkedIn profile. The more you add, the more chance it can help you get the job you want. Ten 1% items add up to 10%. So add languages, certifications, organisations you've been a member of (at university or outside), volunteering work and any awards. Even add some interests – it could be karate, violin or films – as employers are interested in hiring well-rounded people who can fit into teams and work with other people. Plus you never know when someone you meet might share an interest, which could be useful in building relationships.

Charles Hardy, Higher Education Leader, LinkedIn

All of the top 100 graduate recruiters will have a LinkedIn page, but by placing yourself in this marketplace you are also accessing small and medium-sized enterprises (SMEs) that generally do not advertise using mainstream medium as their budget is limited.

Social media is the perfect tool for them as they can reach their target audience with minimal cost and effort. Advertising a role on LinkedIn does not require creative ads or copy. A small business can merely state that they are seeking a marketing manager or business development adviser.

This creates a great opportunity for graduates as the competition for these posts are limited. As stated earlier, for every one position on a graduate scheme an employer receives on average 68 applications. Due to the limited availability of budget and time to advertise, small businesses present a good option to not only seek employment but also to develop your skills.

brilliant dos and don'ts

What to do and not do when creating a LinkedIn profile
- ✔ Make sure you have the right photo – professional and friendly.
- ✔ Have a great headline and summary – first impressions are critical, as well as clarity on who you are and what you want to do.
- ✔ Complete as many sections of your profile as you can – the more you have, the better your chances.
- ✗ Don't write too much – loads of words put people off, so be concise and to the point.
- ✗ Don't lie or exaggerate your qualifications or experience – you will be found out.
- ✗ Don't include anything that might be confidential.

Charles Hardy, Higher Education Leader, LinkedIn

LinkedIn provides a valuable source of information to help you be successful in your applications. Members of your alumni may now work with the company you want to apply for a position. As a result, they could provide you with an insight into what the company are looking for, and even help you build your network while you are at university.

Whenever a guest speaker, graduate employer or alumni comes to present, link with them on LinkedIn. You never know where it might lead. They may be able to provide you with advice on the structure of your CV or insights into how to find your first graduate role. When you read your connections profiles, you may also find that there are people in their network who they can refer you to. They may just know someone who could help you in your job search. This is an excellent opportunity for your connection to introduce you to someone in their network.

Widening your network is such a great advantage as every time you connect to a professional, it brings you one step closer to accessing their network. When you search for individuals LinkedIn provides you with a summary of how you are connected, and advises you on how you are linked to individuals through your connections.

Using LinkedIn as a networking tool

Opportunities are tied to people. 'It's not what you know, it's who you know' is still very relevant today. Having the right connections can help you access information and jobs you might not otherwise find. Start by connecting to people you know – and you probably know more people than you think you know – friends, people on your course and in your lectures, people on teams or groups with you, tutors, managers, family and family friends.

Many of these might not seem like important or relevant connections right now, but you don't know the future and where these people will end up working, where their careers will take them. It could be that in two years' time you discover that someone off your course (who you have not kept in touch with, but you did connect to on LinkedIn) is now working at a company you are about to apply to. And they can maybe give you some help with information, insight, maybe even a referral (that could get them a bonus).

Or you might discover that a relative is connected to someone at that company. You just don't know, so be positive and proactive in growing your network and connecting to everyone you know and meet as you go along.

Connections are not endorsements. Just because I'm connected to someone, I'm not necessarily saying they are amazing at their job; we're just connected and that might be useful for me or them at some point in time. Sometimes you may want to invite people who you do not know well, which is ok in specific occasions as long as you provide some context or an explanation on why you want to connect with them. In this instance you should always personalise the invitation message. Make sure you click 'Connect' from their profile page (on Desktop) and you will see the box where you can write your personal message.

For example: 'Dear Charles, it was great to meet you at the Careers Fair at Bath last week. I was really interested to hear about the exciting opportunities at XYZ. Please can we connect and you direct me to more information? Thanks, Zoe.'

This will give you a much higher chance of a positive response.

Networking isn't just about inviting and connecting to people. It's also about being a useful connection. By sharing useful content, articles, links and blogs to your connections, you are adding value – and you are enhancing your own brand at the same time. You want people to think that you can offer interesting information and you are a useful contact. Your professional brand is about how you act and engage others, not just what is in your profile or CV.

Facebook

Facebook presents another opportunity for students to engage with companies and find out more about what they do. Many of the graduate recruiters and small and medium-sized enterprises have a Facebook page where they promote information about the organisation, and openings as and when they arise.

Students need to ensure that their profile is presentable and demonstrates the kind of employee a company would want to hire. If your Facebook page is filled with drunken nights out make sure you have security settings set to private so if companies search for you, you are seen in the best light. Companies have been known to rescind offers after checking a future employee's Facebook profile. Drunken photos, obscene comments and illegal activity should not be displayed on your profile if you are now beginning to look for work.

If in doubt, do a Google search on your name and check your online profile. Just as on LinkedIn you should join professional groups and get involved with the discussion. This way you can show employers that you are engaged and passionate about the topic, and have a thirst to know more.

You never know who might be part of that network. If you are deciding to use Facebook as a tool to find a graduate role or an internship provide key details about your professional skills, but also keywords so that if employers are searching for individuals with your skills set they can find you.

brilliant tip

Five top tips for using Facebook for job-hunting

- Create a professional profile. If necessary, create two so you can create a clear divide between you socially and professionally.
- Follow the companies you wish to target on your job hunt.

▶

- Use keywords related to your profession so employers can find you.

- Ensure the security settings are set to private on your social profile if it contains content that does not show you in the best light.

- Join networks related to your areas of interest and comment on posts and share relevant content.

How you use Facebook in your job search is not just limited to your profile. Show your passion by incorporating your views on current affairs in your industry. By building a following you may also draw attention from prospective employers. A blog can also be distributed via your Twitter account or LinkedIn page to further expand the reach of your post.

Make sure that your posts are not only entertaining but also provide valuable insights to challenges and changes within the industry. Position yourself as someone, who has a good understanding of the industry and develop relevant recommendations based on valid facts.

Video has become increasingly popular on Facebook and other social media platforms, so this is another medium to demonstrate your understanding of the industry. Find useful video clips developed by industry professionals, news reporters or announcements from companies. Share these clips to establish your brand as an expert in your field. Build your users on the usefulness of your content. Companies will be able to gauge your passion for the industry by the relevance of your posts and the insights provided.

▶ brilliant example

Finding a job through Facebook

I found my first graduate role on Facebook. After meeting a business owner at a networking event I began to follow their company page. I also linked with the owner via LinkedIn. The company was always posting exciting news about the company and how it was growing. I would comment on their posts and congratulate them on their achievements. It looked like a fun place to work and the owner seemed really cool too.

One day the company posted an opening for an entry-level marketing position. As I expected, the application form was not your standard questions. The first question asked me to write about my skills in the format of a tweet. The second question asked me to create a two-minute video about why they should hire me.

I used this opportunity to apply my skills to the recent developments within the company and made recommendations for further growth. After I submitted my application I noticed that the owner had viewed my profile on LinkedIn. You can imagine my surprise when he was the one conducting the interview. We talked about the business and he was impressed with my knowledge about its growth and the market. I received a call that evening to say I was hired so interacting with the company online really paid off.

Twitter

Twitter is another social media platform where employers post information about their company, industry and opportunities. Use your Twitter account to not only engage with companies but to keep abreast of news about your industry. Companies tweet about their company as well as changes, challenges and opportunities that are occurring. As a result, students can become commercially aware by following the leading organisations within their sector.

As with LinkedIn and Facebook, use this as an opportunity to engage with the company and post relevant comments, articles and videos. This will help you to gain followers who are also interested in the sector. They will share your tweets and posts. Through this level of interaction, you will become more aware about developments within the company and can keep abreast about future openings.

YouTube

YouTube hosts many videos and channels delivered by companies offering advice to students preparing to search for a new career opportunity. Companies also post videos of employees who provide a great opportunity to gain an insight into what it is like to work for them.

It also serves as a platform for you to allow companies to find out more about you. Create a video CV highlighting your skills and passions, but more importantly what value you could add to an organisation. This is your opportunity to create your individual brand: what makes you stand out?

brilliant recap

- The majority of companies have a LinkedIn, Facebook or Twitter page to promote information about their company and opportunities.

- Small and medium-sized business often only use social media to advertise openings at their companies.

- Follow companies you are interested in on LinkedIn, Facebook and Twitter.

- Join groups related to your industry and get involved in the discussion.

- Create a professional profile by choosing a professional photo, personalising the headline, using keywords associated with the types of careers you are interested, using the summary on LinkedIn to promote your potential. Complete all of the sections.

- Build your network on LinkedIn, Facebook and Twitter.

- Share and post useful articles and information.

- If you have pictures on your Facebook page that don't present you in a good light, change your settings to private.

- Follow a company's Facebook page.

- Comment on posts or develop relevant posts about the industry or sector.

- Create a video CV to promote your brand.

- Google your name and see if your online profile matches the true you.

CHAPTER 6

Career planning

If you are going to invest £50,000 in a product, you had better know how to use it.

Planning your career is not an easy task. How do you know if a career is for you just by reading about it? The reality of career planning is that you will never know if you have chosen the right career or company until you start working there.

Every career has clear indicators profiling the types of characters who would enjoy working in that particular role. Do not ignore these profiles as they will help you identify suitable careers and your careers service will have a number of tools to help you choose. Your degree will also be an indicator of whether you would enjoy working in roles related to your discipline. Having a good understanding of your goals and aspirations is a key starting point.

Self-assessment

Knowing YOU is the first step to being able to identify a career. You need to understand your likes and dislikes before you can make any decisions. Do you operate well under stress? Do you like working with customers or prefer computers? Do you like to travel or do your personal commitments limit your time away from home? What are your strengths and weaknesses?

If you have a good understanding of yourself, you are better placed to find a career that fits your needs. The careers service will have a range of diagnostic tools for you to use, but there are some simple exercises you can do to understand what's important to you.

How to choose a career that's right for you

Or, what do I want to do when I grow up? To be honest, this
is a difficult one as most people will end up having a number
of different careers over their working lives and can end up in
roles that they didn't realise existed in sectors that they hadn't
considered. The best approach is to be open-minded and not be too
fixed on a particular sector. So research roles that you are interested
in and fit your skill set across the board.

Also in today's highly competitive market look for opportunities
that get your foot in the door. For example, if you are interested in
securing an accountancy role in a particular sector or organisation it
could be easier to get a finance-related job, such as administration
in the finance section in the first instance and look for opportunities
from within. As 99% of the employers in the UK are small and
medium-sized enterprises (SMEs) target these and don't just consider
the industry giants. The London Stock Exchange Group Report –
1000 Companies to Inspire Britain (http://www.lseg
.com/resources/1000-companies-inspire-britain) could be a good
starting point. You could also use TARGETjobs careers planner
(https://targetjobs.co.uk/careers-report) report to find out which
graduate jobs would suit you.

How to research career opportunities

Look on university websites (not just your own university's) and see
the destinations of leavers from your course or programme of study.
Use LinkedIn to track graduate outcomes from your institution and
course as well as alumni you can contact for information.

Consult websites such as Career Player or Career Box for further
information and the Guardian UK 300 based on graduate careers

and employment. Talk to people as very often people stumble on a career and don't actually plan it. Let them describe their route into their particular career. Go to lectures or meetings at professional bodies, attend events at your local chamber of commerce and network. You will be surprised at how much information people are prepared to share about their personal journeys when asked. You can always arrange to meet up with them at a later date to find out more about them and their role.

How to gain experience while studying at university

Take up every opportunity that is available at your university from year one. Join or run a society or club, be a student ambassador, volunteer, be mentored or volunteer to mentor students at a college or secondary school, take on responsibility at your local faith group and try to work every summer – it doesn't matter what you do, just do something.

Look out for opportunities to work on campus through your university's careers or employment team. If you want to develop skills through studying abroad, check if your university offers the Erasmus study abroad scheme.

All these things will develop skills alongside your studies that employers value and will give you something to talk about at an interview.

Femi Bola, Director of Employability, University of East London

Personal review

Another means is to conduct a self-assessment by viewing yourself through the eyes of others. A personal review allows you to gain insight from those you work with on a professional and informal basis. Rate yourself and then ask a minimum of five people, who know you in different capacities, to rate you. Are you as brilliant as you thought?

Don't take the results to heart, but use them as a means to gain an insight into you and to develop an action plan. Often we don't see our strengths or we don't take credit for the things we do, so a personal review helps us to gain another perspective.

Use the table below to carry out your own personal review.

Traits and skills valued by employers	1	2	3	3	4	5
Punctual						
Reliable						
Attention to detail						
Problem-solving						
Communication (oral and written)						
Numerate						
Innovative						
Positive attitude						
Honest						
Meet deadlines						
Accurate						
Can think on your feet						
Organised						
Team player						
Leader						
Negotiator						
Influencer						

Name one strength:
Name one weakness:

brilliant examples

The value of a personal review

The personal review presented a few surprises. My scores were so much lower than the people I asked to review me. They had a much higher opinion of me and identified my strengths and weaknesses. It was a good exercise to see myself through the eyes of my friends and colleagues.

A psychology graduate

Developing an action plan

Employability is a journey and it is important to recognise that you will be continuously developing and honing your skills. The journey is never-ending if you wish to continue to be employable, as the market is forever changing. Therefore based on the feedback you receive or the potential career you wish to enter, develop an action plan to address either areas of weakness or areas where you lack knowledge about potential careers.

Use the action plan below to develop your weaknesses.

Skill, attribute or area to be researched	Why are these skills or attributes important?	Action to be taken (show how you will develop the skill)	How will you demonstrate your skill?	Date for completion
Example: team work	In the workplace you will be required to work in teams	Join student society or sports team	Take on a specific function to draw on examples of specific actions taken	End of academic year

Exploring your career

The best way to find out about a career is to either speak to a professional in the sector or secure a place on an internship or insight day. Speaking with professionals and learning about their journey can help you reflect on whether this is the path you wish to take. They can give you an insight into the possibilities in the sector and within their organisation. They can also provide you with an idea about the culture of the organisation, which you simply cannot gain from reading about an organisation.

Joining professional bodies or networking at industry events is a great way to meet people who are working in your chosen careers. Every discipline relates to a professional body that often has a student membership section. Google your discipline and type in professional body and you should be able to find the body that relates to your studies.

Here are some examples of professional bodies:

● The Chartered Institute for IT: http://www.bcs.org/
● The Chartered Institute of Marketing: http://www.cim.co.uk/

brilliant action

Join a professional body

● It provides an opportunity to network with practising professionals both online and face to face.
● Most professional bodies will offer real-world career advice and opportunities for continuing professional development.
● It offers access many of the same resources that industry professionals use.
● It shows that you are serious about a career in your chosen profession.
● When applying for your dream job it just might give you an edge with potential employers.

Philip Preston, Network Manager,
The Chartered Institute of Marketing

Insight days

Many organisations run insight days, challenges or open days for students to understand more about their organisation and to meet recent graduates who can tell them more about possible career paths and opportunities with the organisation. They are also a great opportunity to ask questions about the application process and what the company are looking for in new recruits.

brilliant action

Attend an insight day

Industry insight days are also a useful way of finding out how an industry or sector currently operates and the range of roles available. Such days give you the opportunity to see how a role that you might be considering is represented in a particular sector, e.g. an HR role in a technology or construction company or an accountancy role in a health setting.

Companies often use recent graduates as ambassadors at insights days so you can find out from someone just a little further on in their career what they studied, how they secured their role and the benefits of working for a particular employer. Such days are also great for networking so pick up as many business cards as you can and make sure that you follow up leads as quickly as possible to request further information or a meeting.

Femi Bola, Director of Employability, University of East London

brilliant example

Challenges with MyKindaFuture

MyKindaFuture offers a one-stop-shop for businesses looking to connect with, train and recruit students across secondary, further and higher education. It specialises in helping students develop employability skills, while supporting employers with their specific recruitment needs across the board – from work experience and apprenticeships through to graduate programmes.

▶

It connects students with businesses through meaningful face-to-face engagement and distinct online challenges which inspire students and help them understand different career routes, sectors and disciplines. The organisation works with over 70 leading businesses across a wide range of sectors.

Emma O'Connor, Senior Marketing and
Communications Manager, MyKindaFuture

Online career-planning resources

Prospects (www.prospects.ac.uk) is the official graduate careers website. It includes a prospects planner, which serves as a resource for students to research and read about prospective careers. The tool helps students recognise their skills and understand how they translate into potential career paths. There is information specifically related to degree disciplines and useful tools to research career options. The prospects planner is an extensive resource to explore career opportunities based on your skills and ambitions.

Other useful websites include:

- Careerplayer: http://www.careerplayer.com/
- Targetjobs: https://targetjobs.co.uk/
- Gradjobs: https://www.gradjobs.co.uk/

brilliant impact

Two innovative apps

Debut is a disruptive careers mobile app dedicated to students and graduates. Debut's mission is to change the way students and graduates learn about, find and secure their ideal careers by using mobile technology. The innovation of the product lies in the fact that it reverses the recruitment flow by bringing employers to the students and bypassing the traditional application process.

Debut is open to students in the UK and abroad and enhances access to careers for students from all different backgrounds by providing direct access to employers. Students can easily create a profile by providing basic information about themselves, their educational background and their careers preferences. These data allow Debut to match students with opportunities such as insight days, internships, graduate programmes and so on.

Through its flagship feature, the Talent Spot, employers are able to directly contact students with personalised opportunities. Talent Spots could contain invitations to events, phone interviews or even fast-track opportunities to be placed straight into the final assessment centre or interview. By using data Debut can help many students bypass the arduous application and psychometric testing phases of the recruitment process.

On Debut students can also play sponsored mobile games to learn more about certain employers and compete to win career-related prizes that include internships.

The Debut app is free to download and is available for both iOS and Android.

Michele Trusolino, COO of Debut

PathMotion transforms an established recruitment practice – conversations between candidates and employees – into a disruptive and cost-effective online solution. It gives candidates a deeper and more effective level of engagement with prospective employers. As many as 96% of candidates would like to talk with employees of their target firms. In the past, candidates were limited to their network or to attending career fairs or events to meet employees. With PathMotion candidates can attend dedicated live chat events or select employees online based on university or current job and ask them questions.

All previous discussions are available online and benefit all candidates and are search engine optimised. This means candidates and employees can exchange at a time and in a location that is convenient for them, making best use of their time while creating useful content for the benefit of other candidates.

Keith Quesenberry confirms in the Harvard Business Review that 'people are attracted to stories, because we're social creatures and we relate to other people'.

The role that storytelling can play in responding to candidates' search for authenticity should come as no surprise. While job seekers can access many facts about a target employer, facts alone are unlikely to be sufficient to answer many burning questions. Candidates' engagement activity on the platform helps PathMotion understand their interests which it can then use to tailor their experience and use to their benefit.

Jonathon Deakin, Client Director, PathMotion

Career goals: blue-sky thinking

In your ideal world, when you graduate, what position do you see yourself in? Now work backwards to identify actions to achieve that goal. How can you identify what actions you need to take? Use industry profiles of the skills desired by employers in your chosen career, assess yourself against those skills and identify areas for development. Your personal review will also highlight areas for development.

Regardless of your chosen career path, employers will have generic and specific skill sets they require in their candidates. As a result, it is important to understand the criteria against which you will be measured when you graduate. Develop both short- and long-term objectives to ensure your success. Use your own self-assessment, the results of your personal review and employer's requirements for the role you wish to pursue to develop an action plan. These objectives should be SMART:

Specific	What do you want to achieve and by when?
Measurable	How will you know you have achieved your goal?
Achievable	What are the actions or tasks needed to achieve success?
Realistic	Is it likely you can achieve this goal in the timeframe specified?
Timely	Give yourself a deadline

Your goals in your first year may focus on researching the options available to you with your degree discipline. There may be careers you have not considered, as many graduate schemes are not discipline-specific and so you may study psychology but find yourself working in an investment bank.

In your first year, one goal may be to explore possible career options, and the actions involved in achieving this goal could be researching information about possible careers via the university careers service or developing your generic employability skills through extracurricular activities.

In your second year you may begin to focus on identifying means to gain an internship, noting the deadlines for applications and identifying possible companies.

When you reach your final year, your focus will be on identifying graduate schemes and companies you wish to apply to, as well as opportunities to meet with these companies at graduate fairs and open days and networking with previous graduates to learn from their experiences.

It is essential that you set yourself goals and tasks as your time at university will pass very quickly. Use the table below to develop a set of goals for your time at university and the actions to achieve them.

Don't worry if your career goals change. At university you will be exposed to new opportunities and experiences, which will undoubtedly have an impact on you as a person and ultimately your aspirations. This is all part of the development process and will ensure that upon graduation you have a better understanding of YOU.

Overall career goal

Year 1	Action	Outcome
Goal 1		
Goal 2		
Goal 3		
Year 2		

(continued)

Overall career goal
Goal 1
Goal 2
Goal 3
Year 3
Goal 1
Goal 2
Goal 3

brilliant recap

- Knowing YOU – your strengths, your weaknesses, your likes and dislikes – is the first step in choosing a career.

- Identify what is important to you – travel, flexibility, money or career progression?

- Research career options by networking with industry professionals or attending employer events, where you can pose your questions to the company directly.

- Join the professional body linked to your chosen career or discipline.

- Network with the alumni of your course to learn from their experiences.

- Use a personal review to learn how you are perceived by others and identify areas for development.

- Explore online resources and apps.

- Create an account on the Prospects website (www.prospects .ac.uk) and use the prospects planner to map your career.

- Develop an action plan for your three years of study to develop the skills required upon graduation.

- Define SMART career goals and the actions needed to achieve them.

CHAPTER 7

Finding a job

Invest time in developing
employability skills while studying,
so upon graduation you can
harvest the return on your
investment

The fact that you are reading this book shows you are interested in improving your chances of employment upon graduation. The Graduate Market in 2016 by High Fliers Research highlighted two important facts:

- Almost half the recruiters who took part in the research repeated their warnings from previous years – that graduates who have had no previous work experience at all are unlikely to be successful during the selection process and have little or no chance of receiving a job offer for their organisations' graduate programmes.
- Recruiters have confirmed that 32% of this year's entry-level positions are expected to be filled by graduates who have already worked for their organisations, either through paid internships, industrial placements or vacation work.

The importance of gaining work experience at university has become a prerequisite for finding employment upon graduation. Job shadowing, internships and placements have become increasingly important.

Placements and internships

Taking a placement is an opportunity to integrate the academic theory from your course with practice while developing your transferable skills and competencies. Employers increasingly expect graduates to understand industry culture and have commercial awareness, and this is hard to do without work experience.

You will increase your self-confidence, motivation to succeed and your sense of professionalism.

Applying for a placement gives you the chance to experience the job application process, including interviews and assessment centres, and will put you in a much better position when it comes to securing a graduate-level job.

It's a great way to have a clearer understanding of what career you want, all the time developing your personal network of career and industry contacts. Placements can be totally transformative to your outlook on your studies as they offer the opportunity to earn money, travel and start to become the early career professional you want to be on graduation.

brilliant tip

How to find a placement

- Make frequent and full use of your university or college careers service.
- Pick up volunteering or work shadowing experience to give you something to talk about on your application form.
- Develop a digital identity to be proud of – if someone searches for you online they will find positive results and not things you would be embarrassed by.
- Sign up for vacancy listing services both in your university or college, and by external boards.
- Practise your interview skills, get feedback on your applications and be persistent.

Sarah Flynn, Chair of ASET

ASET, the work-based and placement learning association, aims to advance the prevalence, effectiveness and quality of work-based and placement learning in higher education.

Types of work experience

There are many opportunities to undertake work experience while at university. Some are competitive to secure, but the opportunities do exist. Opportunities vary depending upon your level of study. Below is a list of various types of work experience offered by companies.

Job shadowing

Job shadowing is often unpaid, but provides an opportunity to observe a professional at work in their work setting. You gain an insight into the daily tasks and responsibilities involved in a particular role. You can pose questions about your career choices and decide whether or not this really is the career for you. It can be undertaken in any year of study and used to explore various career options.

Internships

Internships can vary in length but are often for a fixed period ranging from 3–12 weeks and take place during the Easter or summer holiday. You can gain an insight into the culture of the organisation, the specifics of the role and, more importantly, you can form a view on whether you are suited to the role or not.

Students are allocated to a supervisor who will assign them a range of tasks and projects. Internships also provide an opportunity to network within the organisation, which can prove useful in the future.

Placements

Placements provide students with a rotation to various departments within the organisation. Companies often target students in their penultimate year of study or those who have recently graduated. Placements are longer in duration and often last for 6–12 months. Students can undertake a placement as part of their course or during a gap year. Placements often form the basis of the final-year dissertation, providing students with an opportunity to research a real issue faced by an organisation or industry.

You can gain an insight into the company, build a useful network and also review career options. If your placement is successful, the company may invite you to join the company following graduation.

---

brilliant example

A graduate recruiter's view of internships

The early careers market is evolving at an alarming rate, students are more switched on than ever before and the competition for early engagement to secure the top talent has really heated up among organisations.

Internships provide us with a great opportunity to pipeline talent into our business from as early as the first year and hopefully then create a relationship that translates into future graduate positions.

From a student's perspective it's a great way to really experience the culture of an organisation, and gain valuable experience in the workplace. We absolutely use our internship and industrial placements as a pipeline into graduate opportunities.

Helen Alkin, Head of Future Talent Recruitment,

Marks and Spencer plc

Despite the vast range of opportunities presented in the table below, with 90% of the UK's top employers offering some form of work experience, the market is still increasingly competitive. If students wish to undertake work experience, they need to do their research.

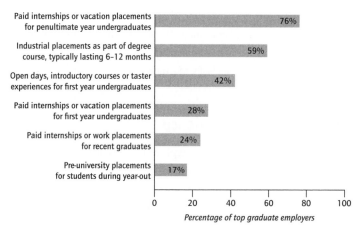

Paid internships or vacation placements for penultimate year undergraduates — 76%
Industrial placements as part of degree course, typically lasting 6–12 months — 59%
Open days, introductory courses or taster experiences for first year undergraduates — 42%
Paid internships or vacation placements for first year undergraduates — 28%
Paid internships or work placements for recent graduates — 24%
Pre-university placements for students during year-out — 17%

Percentage of top graduate employers

Source: The Graduate Market, High Fliers Research, 2016

 action

Do a year out in industry

Here are five things you'll get out of a year in industry:

- **Work experience:** The experience you gain through a year in industry will be invaluable – not only for your future job prospects, but as transferrable skills for your degree.

- **Communication:** Emojis and text speak won't cut it in the corporate world. By being immersed in that environment you'll learn how you can adapt your communication across phone conversations, emails and face-to-face meetings, as well as the difference between internal and external communication. So remember, when applying, keep it formal.

- **Using people's knowledge:** You're not expected to know everything and hit the ground running. You will be expected to learn quickly and get stuck in.

- **Work/life balance:** University is a lot of fun. You have to study, but a lot of time is leisure. During your year placement you'll learn how to balance your business responsibilities as well as your life.

● **Life skills:** Budgets may not sound like fun but they're definitely
something you need to know about. With rent, council tax and travel
you'll learn pretty quickly how to manage your money.

Alex Field, Marketing Manager, RMP Enterprise

How to find work experience

Knowing the career you wish to explore is a starting point for identifying work experience opportunities. Research into your chosen
career will highlight companies you may wish to work for and their
websites will provide information about possible work experience.

Your search will be more targeted and focused if you have an idea
of the company you wish to work for and the careers you wish to
explore.

 example

Magnet.me: An innovative way to discover opportunities

If you're not aware of a company, how are you ever going to work there?
Magnet.me aims to connect students with possible career paths by showing
them opportunities at both the well-known big corporations and companies
they may have never heard of before.

Magnet.me is pretty simple. As a student you can easily create a profile
by filling in your CV, with your education, work experience and skills. From
there on, Magnet.me does most of the work. You will receive suggestions of
potential companies to work for based on your profile and their criteria. In
that way, you quickly gain a vast network of potential employers that meet
your interests (and you know you meet their criteria).

This network of companies fuels your personalised newsfeed that consists
of all new career opportunities, events and company updates. Magnet.me
also has many cool features to make job-seeking journey even better. You

can take a sneak peek inside companies' offices by scrolling through the photos on their company page, or like their timeline updates through which you can get noticed by recruiters.

Magnet.me helps you take the first steps of your career and discover your ideal internship or job.

Vincent Karremans, Founder and Managing Director, Magnet.me

Use the careers service

The careers service at your university should be the first place you visit when trying to find an internship, placement or graduate role. You are not the first student to graduate from your course, so use its experience for their knowledge of recruiters, what they require, deadlines and opportunities.

Careers services often have websites where positions are posted, so register to receive alerts to your email address. (Do remember to check your inbox daily and respond to emails in a timely manner.)

brilliant example

Summer work experience with Shell

At Shell I was placed in the treasury department where I was responsible for updating the credit reports for 20 different Shell-owned entities. I had to use the company's most recent financial statement and identify the relevant figures to input into Moody's risk calculator. After I received a credit rating I would then compare this rating with their previous rating and discuss the results and the reasons for change with various treasury managers.

At the end of my three weeks I had to present my findings to all the treasury managers and my line manager. I learnt various skills in the process, including being more analytical, and now having a better ability to quickly read and process financial statements. I can also present my findings clearly and concisely.

As I completed all 20 reviews, I believe I developed the ability to deliver projects in the timeframe set and to the highest standard.

Michael Rene, Business Management with
Economics Undergraduate

 example

Work experience in a marketing role

I attended a talk at the Chartered Institute of Marketing, where the speaker, Misa von Tunzelman from JLL, was talking about her career. This was the moment that I was not only attracted to marketing as a subject but had a hunger to find out more about JLL. After the talk I approached Misa and asked if we could meet for a coffee, as I would like to learn more about a career in marketing. To my surprise Misa gave me her card. I emailed her the next day and her assistant booked me into her diary. Our talk allowed me to gain an insight into the world of marketing, but also Misa was just so friendly I did not feel nervous at all.

I was therefore so excited when I was able to gain work experience at JLL. Enlightening, exhilarating and enjoyable are the three words I would use to describe my time there. I provided support for the JLL Property Triathlon, and also interviewed managers and rotated around areas of the organisation to learn more about marketing roles. A great experience. This opportunity was only possible due to me stepping out of my comfort zone at the CIM event. I would definitely advise students to attend professional body events, as it is a great opportunity to meet professionals in your desired field.

Melodie Trought, University of Sussex

The websites below are other useful resources for internship opportunities:

- Inspiring Interns: www.inspiringinterns.com
- Employment for Students: www.e4s.co.uk
- Prospects: www.prospects.ac.uk/work_experience.htm
- Graduate Talent Pool: http://graduatetalentpool.direct.gov.uk
- RateMyPlacement: www.ratemyplacement.co.uk
- Target Jobs: http://targetjobs.co.uk

brilliant tip

How to find internship opportunities

When looking for an internship don't just consider the usual suspects, the well-known corporates that run huge annual recruitment campaigns that are highly competitive and attract thousands of applicants.

Internships in sectors such as retail which are not considered so attractive can provide a wide range of hands-on experience, including staff management, customer care, money management, stock handling and control, skills and experience that easily transfer to other sectors.

Look at websites such as RateMyPlacement (www.ratemyplacement.co.uk) to gain an insight into what graduates have said about internship employers across a number of sectors. Consider using LinkedIn to trace alumni from your university to approach for opportunities. Your university's careers and employability service should also have a list of live internship opportunities for you to make use of.

Finally, if appropriate look out for internships aimed at addressing inequalities by targeting specific groups such as women, students with disabilities or those from Black, Asian and minority ethnic backgrounds.

Femi Bola, Director of Employability, University of East London

Your chance to demonstrate your employability skills

Applying for an internship, placement or graduate role is your chance to test your product in a live environment. The feedback you gain from your application, interviews or assessment centres will help you fine-tune your product.

Do you need to increase your skill set, or do you have the skills but your communication does not lend itself to marketing your features and strengths? Completing an application form and communicating your skill is an art and takes practice.

Review the skills identified in the I Brand employability model to see how you can best demonstrate your ability and aptitude for a role. Review all your extracurricular activities and the tasks completed on your degree and identify the best examples to support your application. Your involvement with voluntary work, sports or academic study will provide examples to strengthen your application.

Review the employability skills developed on your degree. Then complete the table below, highlighting the various skills you have developed and how they relate to the skills you need to be successful in the application process. Employability is built into the assessment methods, so it's important to communicate how you have developed specific skills by completing your assessment.

Once you have reviewed your skills, look at your development as a result of your involvement with extracurricular activities. Highlight how your skills are relevant to the role, making specific reference to tasks or activities where you took the lead, showed initiative or negotiated a better rate.

Assessment method	Employability skills	Relevance to role
Extracurricular activities	Skills used and developed	Relevance to role

brilliant tip

Don't be afraid of the letter 'I'

All too often students review activities in the plural, saying or writing 'We did this and we did that'. 'We' are not applying for a role so it is important to highlight the 'I' – *your* role in completing the tasks and *your* contribution.

As highlighted in the I Brand employability model, your contribution will be unique. I Brand urges students to reflect on their skill set and personal traits, which ultimately define what makes you stand out.

So refer back to the I Brand employability model and consider what specific skills you used or developed as a result of completing the task. Are you a strong project manager or good team player? In relation to your I Enterprise, were you innovative in your approach and how did you persuade your team members to adopt your suggestions? Have you undertaken presentations or report writing in the past and so were able to draw on your individual experiences to share with the group members?

Creating your I Brand is an individual process so no brands will be the same. It is not sufficient to develop the skills. Students need to also develop their I Marketing skills to ensure that their brand is communicated effectively in their application and in personal appearance.

Companies spend millions developing their brands and the qualities associated with them. As a new product – a graduate in the market – you need to invest the time to define the essential elements of your brand. Once you are able to define your brand, it will be easier to identify how your skills will be marketable in the graduate job market.

Work experience with small and medium-sized enterprises

SMEs represent an excellent opportunity for students to gain a wide range of exposure to business processes, roles and responsibilities. The very nature of an SME's structure can provide students with opportunities to be exposed to far more responsibility than within a larger organisation.

In an SME roles are not as compartmentalised into departments, so there are more opportunities for you to excel and take on more responsibility. But only if you are good. The recruitment process in an SME is also more informal and so reduces the number of hurdles to secure a role.

---

brilliant example

Placement review of an engineering industrial placement

Salary: £16,000–£17,999

Roles: Chemical Engineering, Chemistry, Engineering, Food science, Pharmaceutical

Course: BEng Chemical Engineering

To what extent did you enjoy your work placement or internship?

I enjoyed working in a chemical engineering company. I was placed at one of the smaller sites, which meant I was able to get involved in many functions of the business. I feel I would not have got this same experience had I been placed at one of the larger sites. I got to work across engineering and R&D and was given responsibility for various projects. There has been so much work I have done which will be extremely valuable for my CV.

To what extent did you feel valued by your colleagues?

As part of a smaller site, I got to work with almost all of my colleagues. They have shown me that I am a trusted member of the team by involving me in many projects and knowing when to include me so I can learn something new. All of the staff here have been welcoming and friendly since my first day and I really feel like part of the team here.

To what extent were you given support and guidance by management/your supervisors

My manager has a lot of experience in process engineering and it has been fantastic working and learning from him. He has included me in projects to give me the most varied experience and I know that his priority has always been for me to learn the most I can. He has also offered support in applying for future jobs.

How much responsibility were you given during your placement?

I project managed a new product development from development to launch. This was a big responsibility as this product will be sold in shops soon. I was also involved in a lot of business-critical investigations and process developments. I think I was given a lot of responsibility for an intern but I feel like I had to earn that – which is reasonable to expect.

To what extent will the skills you developed, and training you received, assist you in your degree studies and beyond?

I now have so many examples of work I have carried out that I will be able to use when being interviewed for graduate jobs. I have also improved my report writing and leadership skills with the project I have managed. I have learned to be adaptable to different teams and situations too. Working with the supply chain leadership is very different to working with operators and I had to adjust daily to these situations.

Supplied by RMP Enterprise

Temporary to permanent roles

Temporary roles are an excellent way to access an *organisation*. Whether your role is for three or six months, you can use this time to navigate your way around the *organisation* to the department you want to work for. Build a network, offer your services to help, but above all else, shine.

If you can prove your worth, the company may be willing to take you on permanently or extend your contract. Temporary roles also help you to build experience on your CV to secure permanent positions. Securing temporary work is challenging as there is little training and companies expect you to hit the ground running. As a result, recruitment agencies only put forward those candidates who they feel can perform the tasks required and think on their feet.

Companies and organisations usually use recruitment agencies to source temporary staff. Due to the nature of such roles and the fact that very little training is provided, recruiters are looking for competent candidates, people who can present themselves well, think on their feet and adapt to situations.

How can you make your skills more attractive to recruitment consultants?

Temporary roles will usually be centred on administration duties or support functions. Your CV will need to highlight good organisational skills, computer skills, including MS Word and Excel, telephone skills and the ability to work independently.

---

brilliant example

Taking a temporary job

I found it hard to find a graduate position when I graduated and took a temporary position while I was job-hunting. The job was not in the field that I wanted to work in, but I was working for a company in my top ten. I offered to help members of staff with various projects and performed the tasks well, from filing to typing up documents and creating Excel spreadsheets.

I was complimented on the standard of my work and as a result my contract was extended. I used the opportunity to network and look for internal postings of openings within the company. Within six months I was offered a permanent junior role in an area I was interested in joining.

A business studies graduate

Job-hunting for graduate positions

Finding a graduate position will require the same level of skill as hunting for an internship. Identify the companies you wish to work for, research their deadlines for their recruitment processes and complete the applications.

Finding the right company will take time, as each has its own process and set of requirements, but the more detailed your research, the more likely you are to identify the right company. When seeking graduate opportunities, company websites provide great sources of information about the range of positions available, deadlines and the career options. Other resources include sector-specific publications, the Prospects website (www.prospects.ac.uk) and graduate recruitment fairs.

Companies actively seek to recruit students through graduate recruitment fairs, both on campus and in exhibition halls. Details of these fairs are publicised through your careers service and by searching online. Graduate fairs present a great opportunity to speak with the employer and glean any additional information about the company and what companies are looking for in graduates.

brilliant dos and don'ts

What to do and not do when job-hunting

✔ Think about the companies and roles that appeal to you most and investigate them further so you really understand what is expected in the role before applying.

✔ Talk to recent graduates, friends, family and lecturers to determine where you are best focussing your energies.

✘ Don't be tempted to scatter your applications far and wide. You will have more chance of success if you target your applications

▶

to the five or so organisations that you really engage with from a brand perspective and invest time on those applications.

X Don't give up as there are graduate jobs out there.

Helen Alkin, Head of Future Talent Recruitment,

Marks and Spencer plc

Innovative approaches to recruitment

The graduate market has seen many companies attempting to disrupt their recruitment processes to encourage a more diverse range of applicants. In 2015 both PwC and Reed Smith adopted a new approach to their graduate recruitment. Both companies adopted different approaches to encourage applicants from a more diverse pool and also to reduce any barriers that may exist in their processes.

brilliant tip

PwC's approach to graduate recruitment

PwC's intention is simple. We want to recruit the brightest and best people to join our graduate programme, irrespective of their background.

To help us do this we've removed UCAS scores as selection criteria for our undergraduate and graduate opportunities. We're proud to have been the first professional services organisation to do this. We did it to challenge the perception that academic achievement alone is indicative of potential. Graduates with well-rounded employability skills and a passion for our business, client service and a willingness to learn new things are very important to us.

A challenge we have year on year is helping graduates understand that our graduate training programmes are available to students from any degree discipline. We want students who have studied arts and humanities subjects, as much as we do students with accounting and finance degrees. They'll get all the support and training they need to be successful in our business regardless of the degree subject they studied. This approach helps us to be a diverse business and support our clients' complex needs.

We are also working to challenge the view that all graduate opportunities are in London. Over half of our graduate vacancies are in our regional offices and all offer an excellent platform for students to progress and excel in their career. We have 30 offices around the UK.

Here are five top tips for students:

- **Do your research:** Employers have lots of information on their websites to help build your knowledge around what they do, how they do it and the sort of people they're looking for.

- **Go above and beyond:** Visiting an organisation's website is a good starting point. To really stand out attend employer events (either at university or attending an office-based open day event) and find out as much as you can and talk to their recruitment team and recent graduate joiners. When you meet people make sure you ask questions and speak to as many people as possible. A little bit of prior preparation can go a long way to helping you.

- **Practise, practise, practise:** Make sure you prepare for your interview, often the best way of doing this is by practising with a friend or family member or even filming yourself. We have some online e-learns to help you too (www.pwc.com/uk/employability).

- **Demonstrate your employability skills:** Customer service, networking, flexibility and team-working are all real aspects of business life that you might have experienced in your study, work or time out. Academic performance is important but it's not the only thing we look for.

- **Body language in an interview:** A firm handshake, not forgetting to smile and eye contact are some examples of what you need to remember when being interviewed.

Sammie Stapleton, Head of UK Talent Channels, PwC

▶ brilliant example

Strengths-based recruitment at global law firm Reed Smith

At Reed Smith we use strengths-based assessments to recruit our trainee solicitors. This approach is designed to understand what energises and motivates candidates, as well as what they can do well. We have eight key strengths. These were developed in partnership with Capp, following consultation with key stakeholders within the firm about what makes them and our trainee solicitors successful.

Candidates are asked to complete an online situational strengths test (SST). They are given scenarios that they might encounter in the role and asked to prioritise them. Candidates, whether successful or not, receive a feedback report on completing the SST.

If successful, candidates are invited to a face-to-face strengths-based interview (SBI). An SBI is different to a competency-based interview as there are a wide variety of questions (including open-ended and hypothetical), fewer follow-up questions and probing, and the chance for candidates to express how they feel regarding an activity. When preparing for interviews, candidates should think about what their friends and family know them for, what they truly enjoy and the achievements they are proud of and why.

We implemented this approach mainly because it relies less on demonstrating past experience, which can prejudice those from less privileged backgrounds or those with a disability. It also requires candidates to talk about what they enjoy doing, which is generally a positive experience. As we do not disclose the key strengths in advance, responses can't be rehearsed, so we are able to see more of the candidates' real personalities.

We have only been using the new process since 2015, and won't know the full impact until the hires start, two years after recruitment. However, candidates and interviewers speak positively about the new process, and our conversion rate from summer vacation scheme placements to training contract offers has increased by 20%.

Lucy Crittenden, Graduate Recruitment Manager, Reed Smith

Being professional

Being professional is paramount whether students are undertaking an internship, work experience or placement. Students should refer to the company website and research the company values. These values will set the tone of the organisation, so ensure made sure its values are at the forefront of your mind while working there.

brilliant tip

What to do and not do during an internship

- Respect your company's values. More often than not, organisations will have tailored values that represent who they are as a company and how they want to operate. Abiding by these values is crucial as a company uses these when evaluating your behaviour in the office and reflecting on your work ethic.

- Don't be late. Being late is not cool. Arriving 20 minutes after your start time will get you no brownie points with your new employer. Regardless of how long you have worked at an establishment, being late rarely becomes acceptable.

- Don't sit on your phone. Keep that phone in your bag. Facebook, Snapchat and Instagram can wait until after work. Sitting on your phone shows a lack of commitment to the task at hand and has very negative associations.

- Don't assume you know it all. It's easy to get complacent when you become familiar with your day-to-day tasks and workload. There is always a way to improve, new skills to be learned and questions to be asked.

Don't get paralytic at work socials. Socialising at work is definitely encouraged but remember to maintain boundaries when attending corporate events. Know your limits – work socials are for fun but take care and pace yourself. You are representing your company so

▶

composing yourself in a professional manner is vital. Associating your company with vomit and ambulances is not the way to get yourself a golden ticket to jobsville.

Amirah Hajat, Marketing Executive, RMP Enterprise

Have a back-up plan

Due to the increasingly competitive nature of the graduate market, it is important to have a back-up plan if you are unable to secure a position on a graduate scheme. There are many ways to navigate your career and today it is important to exhaust as many options as possible.

Use recruitment and career-specific websites to research opportunities. Your careers service may also be able to help you.

brilliant recap

- Graduates with no work experience will struggle to secure a place on a graduate scheme.
- Of the top graduate employers, 63% offer some form of work experience.
- There are three main types of work experience: job shadowing, internships and placements.
- Companies are offering more opportunities to connect and engage through insight and open days and challenges.
- Small and medium-sized enterprises provide a range of opportunities for students to gain exposure to business processes, roles and responsibilities.
- Do not ignore the value of a temporary role as it can lead to a permanent position.

- Be focused in your search for a graduate position – target specific companies you want to work for.
- Companies are increasingly reviewing their recruitment practices to attract a wider pool of talent.
- Have a back-up plan if you are unable to secure a graduate role.
- Act professionally at all times.

CHAPTER 8

Developing an employable you

Developing employability skills is a never-ending journey with lots of twists and turns, and continual opportunities to explore and discover

n this chapter we review the elements of the I Brand employability model and how you can use it to develop your individual brand to increase your employability. Other factors in your development are also considered, including developing an elevator pitch, mentoring and networking. Each of these elements will add value to your portfolio of skills and increase your chance of success.

The model consists of four levels.

1   Your degree

2   Generic employability skills including:

- leadership
- team-working
- positive attitude
- communication
- problem-solving
- commercial awareness
- numeracy
- computer literacy
- cultural sensitivity

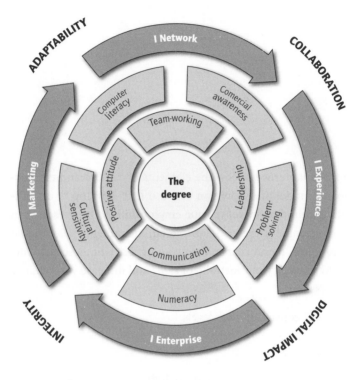

Key

☐ The future

☐ The degree

☐ Generic employability skills

☐ Individual contribution

I Brand employability model

3   Your individual contribution, denoted by:

- I Experience
- I Network
- I Enterprise
- I Marketing

4   Your future

- Collaboration
- Digital impact
- Integrity
- Adaptability

Your degree

There is no doubt that your degree is at the heart of your experience at university, but you also need to recognise the additional layers within the model. Your degree undeniably provides you with a technical and generic skill set that makes you proficient in your field of study, but extracurricular activities can broaden your experience and portfolio of skills.

A degree allows you to enter the arena, but it is your involvement in developing relevant employability skills that will differentiate you from the competition and help you secure a graduate position.

Generic employability skills

The core generic skills outlined in the model give students an indication of graduate recruiters' expectations. These skills are generic in nature and are not industry-specific. They form the basis of standard requirements expected from graduates. As a result, regardless of your discipline, you must be able to provide a practical demonstration of how you have developed these skills through work experience and extracurricular activities.

By actively engaging with the development of these skills you will be able to provide comprehensive examples to support your applications and in interviews for graduate positions.

Use the list of skills below to rate yourself.

Generic employability skills	Definition	Score
Leadership	Self-starter, organisational skills, influencing and motivational skills	
Team-working	Ability to work with others, listen, contribute and negotiate	
Commercial awareness	Understanding key factors that impact business performance and customer satisfaction	
Problem-solving	Provide innovative solutions and recommendations	
Communication	Use oral and written communication effectively	
Numeracy	A general understanding of figures and an ability to manipulate data	
Computer literacy	Basic IT skills and competence in standard IT packages, e.g. Microsoft Office	
Positive attitude	A willingness and drive to try new ideas	

Which of the skills are your strengths and weaknesses? Grade yourself on a scale of 1 to 5 in relation to the skills listed. Now use your scores to develop an action plan with SMART goals to identify how you are going to develop these skills while at university. Complete the table below for each skill.

Goal:
Specific
Measurable
Achievable
Realistic
Timely

Individual contribution

The individual elements of the model recognise a student's individuality. Every student will have a different history and experiences that will separate them so we cannot ignore background and how this impacts, both positively and negatively, on future development. Students also interact with different elements of the model based on personal preferences and personalities and, as a result, no two students can have the same experience.

| Experience

Your individual experiences will impact on how you develop your employability skills. You may be a mature student returning to university to retrain or be the first in your family to attend university, or you may be a single parent. Regardless, you cannot ignore your personal story. Your goals, ambition and drive will dictate to what extent these skills are ingrained into your profile.

| Network

Networking is an essential ingredient when developing employability skills. Your ability to network will help you identify possible job opportunities. How you manage your network, build it and use it is a personal activity. The results of networking will vary for every individual, as the success of networking is dependent upon your ability to develop a rapport and create a memorable impression.

Your network is also based on who you know and their wider network. Some students have the benefit of being able to tap into their parents' network or that of friends. As a result, the extent of your network is also dependent upon your individual connections.

| Enterprise

Entrepreneurial spirit is within you. It is part of your DNA. The ability to find solutions or make recommendations that project a company or product beyond its current constraints is an in-built talent. Entrepreneurial spirit is an individual characteristic and so it is important to recognise that despite the opportunities to develop employability skills, you may or may not be entrepreneurial in your approach.

I Marketing

Ultimately it is how you present yourself to potential employers, both through written and verbal communication, that will determine your ability to secure a position. This ranges from your choice of words to the way you dress to even the way you walk. All of these choices reflect your individual preferences and cannot be replicated by another candidate. As a result, it is important to recognise that, despite having the same employability skills, these will be adopted in different ways and conveyed using different experiences to reflect your individuality.

I Brand

The circular nature of the model indicates the continuous process. Developing your employability skills is continuous. With the advancement of technology, the changing landscape and development of economies have a significant impact on your skills. You can't afford to stand still. Once you secure a position, your next goal is to keep the position.

Updating your skills is an essential part of the current employment climate. Those who let their skills lapse often face redundancy or the need to retrain as their skills become out of date. As a result, you are also continually updating your network, looking for new enterprising ways to conduct business, learning from your experiences and continually updating your brand.

Your future

The world of work is continually changing, spinning faster than our ability to keep up. If you are to maintain your ability to be employable you need to anticipate the direction of change and how it will impact you, your employer and your need for additional skills. The impact of technological change on every aspect of the way we work, live, interact and connect has a far-reaching effect on the way we manage the development of our employability skills.

Technology introduces a level of uncertainty – a level of continued anticipation of what next. It is this backdrop of uncertainty that should propel us into continually questioning whether our current skill set is marketable. Do you have a unique selling point that will allow you to compete for a new position?

Collaboration

Your ability to collaborate will underpin your success. Due to a wide range of skills across multiple disciplines that are needed to complete projects, your success will be determined by your ability to work collaboratively. The connected way in which we work will see teams being formed virtually – and not just in your organisation but in conjunction with other companies and across the globe.

Digital impact

Technology is continually changing, which ultimately impacts on the skills required by industry. The future of your employability skills will be determined by your ability to continually update your skills, but also your ability to identify trends and possible disruptions that will transform your industry. Companies will also favour employees who can translate new technological advancements into new products, services or business processes.

Adaptability

The ability to adapt, to be flexible and resilient are all required. It is not a question of if change is coming but when and how disruptive it will be. If you want to maintain your ability to sell your skills in the marketplace or even just maintain your position with your current employer you need to adapt. Adapting is also about the way we work, where we work and how we work. The only definite aspect of our future is change.

Integrity

All organisations have a set of values, a set of beliefs that they expect their employees to abide by. It is important to ensure you not only know what your values are but that you can demonstrate them in the way you conduct yourself. Integrity also applies to your ability to be professional, your ability to observe and adhere to the rules and processes of your employers. Honesty in today's graduate job market is an attribute valued by employers.

Storytelling

Now you have decided on your individual brand, your strengths and the areas where you excel, how do you communicate all of your greatness to an employer? One way to convey this is by weaving your skills into a well-crafted story. Everyone loves a story, whether it has a good or bad ending. The ability to tell a good story enables you to not only convey the facts to an interviewer but to build a rapport.

 action

Tell your story

- **Create an interesting strap line:** An example of when I overcame a challenge is when. . .
- **Set the scene:** What was your role? What did you do? What did you have to lose? I was winning the race until. . . The project was a success. . .
- **Provide a brief outline of the task:** Paint the picture of the situation for the interviewer. Give them an idea of what was at stake.
- **How you saved the day (or not as the case might be):** Outline your specific actions. What did you do? Show how you used your skills from

your degree, your extracurricular activities, and your personal attributes to complete the task.

● **What was the outcome?:** Stories do not always have a happy ending, so it's perfectly fine if you didn't achieve your goal. Show that you reflected on what you might have done better, and how you would approach the task differently next time.

Lilly Zhang

brilliant question

What advice would you give students to increase their employability while at university?

Extracurricular activities are what set you apart from other candidates. There are thousands of students who finish university at the same time with the same grade, and you will be competing for the same job. That's where extracurricular activities can set you apart from the rest. Whether it be volunteering at a care home, mentoring a secondary school student, completing the London Marathon, being captain at your local football team or being a student representative or ambassador at your university, get involved and know that it's not irrelevant. It shows commitment, passion, leadership skills, ambition – all attributes that any future employer wants to see and hear.

Krystle Siaw, HR Manager, Premier Foods

brilliant tip

How to prepare for the world of work

● Research careers, attend open days, careers workshops and employer talks.
● Develop commercial understanding.

▶

- Undertake work experience or paid employment to help develop transferable skills.
- Build networks both with peers and employers, e.g. use social media such as LinkedIn.
- Be yourself!

Lucy Crittenden, Graduate Recruitment Manager, Reed Smith

Elevator pitch

An elevator pitch is a concise way of stating who you are and what you do, but including an interesting fact about yourself. The reason it is called an elevator pitch is that it denotes the time you have to make an impression between the ground floor and the top floor on an elevator ride. You should be able to introduce yourself within one minute and convey an interesting fact about your skills. Make sure you know your speciality – what makes you unique.

brilliant timesaver

Imagine you get in the lift with an individual you admire. How would you introduce yourself to create an impression? Practise developing a concise introduction stating who you are, what you do and a unique fact about how you perform your job.

Mentors

A mentor is a valuable asset at any point in your career. They can provide an insight into possible career options, offer advice prior to an interview and act as a sounding board for all major decisions. Mentoring can be part of an established programme or an informal relationship.

To make the most of a mentoring relationship, take the time to identify what you hope to gain from the relationship, establish clear goals and aims at the start and schedule all of your meetings for the duration of the programme.

Having an experienced mentor can be a benefit both during and after the programme. If you really connect, your mentor relationship can extend past the mentoring scheme to become part of your personal network.

Building your network

I am bound to everyone on this planet by a trail of six people

Frigyes Karinthy, 1929

A broad network of people will give you an insight into a world of opportunity. Friends of friends will be able to provide you with access to people, information and opportunities. Your network will consist of individuals who are like-minded, but also individuals who would not immediately be seen as your peer. The broader your network, the wider your reach.

Traditional face-to-face networking can involve formal networking events, but also casual conversations over the photocopier. Try not to always see networking as what's in it for you, but look at the wider picture. How can you create situations that will benefit others? Ultimately people will remember you when an opportunity arises that is of interest to you.

Your online network

With the increase of social networking it is just as important to build an online network. LinkedIn provides a platform for social networking with professionals, giving rise to opportunities to connect with alumni, industry professionals and business-related groups. The first step in networking online is to create a LinkedIn profile. (See Chapter 5.)

Your profile is key to networking online as this is how others will find you. LinkedIn can also make it easier for you to not only research companies but also find out about new vacancies. It provides you with an overview of the company and possible opportunities. If anyone in your network works or is connected to the company, it will highlight how you can be recommended through your personal network. This is an excellent mechanism for utilising your network. The discussion groups facilitate discussions with professionals in your chosen career, as well as give you the ability to find out more about career choices.

'Your network is your networth.' This is one of the many slogans thrown around the Elevation Networks office, and one of the charity's founding principles. People don't realise how important networking is until they need something. With six degrees of separation, it is quite possible that your dream employer might be one or two people away from you. LinkedIn is a great example, as it shows you how you may be connected to a total stranger.

Networking allows you to meet potential employers or business partners, gain free advice and develop your communication skills in the process. As a student, you are next in line to fill many of the jobs available, but are you connected enough? Having the right qualifications and experiences is fantastic but sometimes knowing the hiring manager or a director in a certain industry could potentially open up doors. Networking is the key to unlocking unfound opportunities.

✦ brilliant dos and don'ts

What to do and not do when networking
- ✔ Introduce yourself and what you currently do using the elevator pitch technique. Keep it sweet, short and concise.
- ✔ Smile, listen and learn from what is being said. There is so much value in free knowledge.

✔ Follow up with any contacts made within 48 hours. Typically, try to do it in 24 hours but at worst no longer than 48 hours as you will still be fresh in people's mind.

✗ Don't get too personal. You want to build a rapport with the person but it is not the best place to bring up family, finance or friendship issues.

✗ Don't be afraid to ask questions. This is your chance to gain free knowledge and advice so grab this opportunity with both hands.

✗ Don't stick to one person. The whole purpose of networking is to talk to as many people you don't know as possible, so don't just stick to one person or stick with people you know. Even if you feel less confident, you and a friend can approach people together.

Femi Awoyemi, Neet Engagement Coordinator,
Elevation Networks

Opportunities to network

Attending conferences and professional body meetings are a good way to start networking, but there are many more options. Individuals who are passionate about your discipline will create informal networking groups to provide opportunities to network with like-minded professionals.

Eventbrite (www.eventbrite.co.uk/) is a great website to find out about events. Also look for organisations that are linked to your field. A Meetup groups (www.meetup.com) is another avenue to network. Join groups which are directly linked to your career and also those which you are simply interested in finding out more about. There are thousands of Meetup groups and some are more active than others, but it is definitely an opportunity to widen your friendship group and ultimately your network. If you are truly passionate about getting involved, why not start your own Meetup group or organise your own event on Eventbrite.

brilliant example

Make yourself stand out

- It's easy to get lost in the crowd at university when classes can often be lectures addressed to hundreds of students. To stand out, take a proactive role in getting to know your lecturers, especially your advisors. Your professors can be invaluable sources of advice, guidance and networking support in the real world since many of them work or have relationships in the business world as well as the university community.

- Remember your profile information is now out there potentially for everyone to peruse. Prospective employers, networkers and colleagues have access to pictures of you. Remember to keep it appropriate if you are going to use your profile for professional networking.

- Upon joining a professional organisation, consider attending a conference or event sponsored by the group. There you will meet professionals already working in the field who are more than willing to assist the next generation. You may also receive publications from the organisation that list job openings and career advice for young professionals interested in the field.

- Consider creating a networking card. This is simply a business card for people who are not yet in business. A simple card with your name and email address or phone number is all you need.

  - When preparing for your future or developing a professional network, business cards are like golden tickets. Collect business cards when meeting people and always make sure to follow up with an email or letter soon after. Keep the business cards you collect in a safe place for quick and easy reference later on.

- Finding a mentor is especially important at university, when you're at a critical point in your career development. If you can align yourself with people already practising in your selected field, you can learn all kinds of insights that you won't learn in the classroom. When you let it be known that you're looking for someone to help guide you in your career, you may be surprised at how many people offer to lend a hand.

Carol René, Enterprise Lead Information and
Data Architect, Shell International Petroleum Company

brilliant tip

Impress employers with your extracurricular activities

I graduated with a third-class degree, but I still secured a graduate position upon graduation. It was my extracurricular activities that impressed my interviewers. I was able to demonstrate practical examples of employability skills and my achievements.

I had run several successful events at university, helped run the student union radio station and raised £1,000 for charity. What I lacked in a degree, I made up for with my extracurricular activities. Sure, I wish I had graduated with a first, but I am now studying for my Masters.

A human resources management graduate

brilliant recap

- The I Brand employability model defines three layers to developing your employability: the degree, generic employability skills and individual contribution.
- Employability is a continuous cycle as you need to continually update your skills.
- Develop an action plan to identify the skills you need to develop.
- Find a mentor to help navigate both your degree and your career.
- Networking is an excellent way to increase your opportunities as you never know who the people you meet can introduce you to.
- Create a LinkedIn profile as it is important to have an online profile to support your personal networking efforts.

CHAPTER 9

Communicating your employability

Even when you are silent you are still communicating

Always remember, communication is not just verbal. It's also about how you present yourself, the accuracy of your written word, body language and attitude. All of your actions communicate a trait of your professionalism. A badly spelt application speaks volumes about future communications with the company's clients. If you are unable to present yourself in a professional manner, how will you represent the company?

This chapter focuses on opportunities for you to communicate your professionalism in a manner sought after by graduate employers.

CVs, covering letters and application forms

The majority of companies have moved away from receiving CVs in favour of their own application forms. This is primarily to encourage candidates to complete a specific application in response to the company's requirements. (This does not always work, as some candidates still copy and paste responses from one application to another, sometimes without even changing the company's name.)

Companies often find the standard of applications received is better with the use of their own application form. Previously students would not think about the specific role requirements and would send the same CV to several companies in the hope that one would invite them for an interview. The application form in most cases forces students to match their strengths to the requirements of the role they are applying for.

The CV is still an acceptable form of applying for some roles, but also serves as a very useful marketing tool for undergraduates. It encourages students to evaluate their skills in relation to their specific discipline, extracurricular activities and current part-time work and analyse what skills they have developed. Often students feel they have very little to offer, but if you complete the following exercise you will find that throughout your time at university you will have developed a range of skills.

Role	Action	Skills developed
Examples: Saturday sales assistant for three years	Team leader for three members of staff. Organised team shifts, responsible for organising section stock-take and handling customer queries	Commitment, customer service, organisational skills, managerial skills, project management and punctuality

Draw up a table like the one above and see what skills you have developed. Use this information to build your CV.

brilliant example

The value of part-time and voluntary work

It was only when I sat with the careers adviser that I realised I had developed valuable employability skills. I did not see the value in my part-time job or the voluntary work I had been doing for an hour every week for the last two years. This exercise was a real confidence boost, as I had not seen myself in this light before. I had a really clear idea of what I could offer to an employer.

An English graduate

Formatting your CV

A standard CV is two pages in length and contains the following:

- personal details
- contact details
- profile
- educational institution and qualifications (including grades achieved and dates attended)
- work experience in chronological order
- voluntary and extracurricular activities, highlighting achievements
- hobbies and interests.

Here is a good CV checklist:

- Name
- Home and term-time address
- Email
- Mobile
- Profile
- Qualifications listed in chronological order (most recent first)
- Institutions listed
- Dates attended
- Relevant subjects
- Dissertation topic
- Work experience listed in chronological order with summary of duties
- Summary of relevant skills and levels attained
- Summary of key achievements
- Summary of interests.

The table below shows how not to write your CV.

Curriculum vitae G I Sajob Email: darknight@hotmail.com 21 Secret Road London E10 4SU Tel: 020 8123 4567 Mob: 07927 112233	Give your full name. Ensure your contact details are accurate and avoid the use of an unprofessional email address. Record a professional answering message on both numbers.
Personal statement I have worked as a sales assistant for a year and volunteer on Thursdays at the local girl guides.	Your personal statement should be a WOW statement about you – a reason why employers would consider buying your product. Show how your skills are relevant to the role you are applying for. Review the format and fonts used to ensure consistency.
Qualifications GCSE English Lang: B English Lit: A Maths: A* RE: C Science: B PE: B Business Studies: C IT: B A2 Level Economics: B Business studies: A AS Level English: A Economics: B Business Studies: A **Degree:** Economics and Business: 2:1	When listing qualifications, use chronological order with the most recent at the top. Clearly state dates of attendance and the name of the institution. Give details of the main topics covered in your degree, especially those relevant to the role.
Work experience Topshop: Saturday sale assistant B&Q: Store assistant	Clearly state dates of employment. Give an overview of your role, highlighting relevant skills: 'Assisted customers, providing speed and accuracy on the checkout to ensure management of queues and customer satisfaction'. Or 'First line of contact for customers with queries on the shop floor. Resolved customer queries to ensure a good shopping experience'.

(continued)

Interests	How do these interests add value to
Travelling, social networking and reading	your application? Highlight interests that demonstrate your ability to interact, communicate and help others. This area of the application is weak and the student needs to engage in additional extracurricular activity to strengthen the application.
Skills	Highlight skills that are transferable
Strong communication and interpersonal skills	to the world of work. Avoid spelling mistakes as accuracy is essential.
Computer literate	Show which computer skills you have acquired.
References available on request	

Contact details

Avoid using unprofessional email addresses. Either opt to use your university email address or create an online email address that simply uses your name. Do not use the fun email addresses that you use with your friends as such addresses communicate the wrong message to an employer. Always ensure that you check your email on a daily basis, as tardy responses reflect the timeliness of your responses to future clients.

Language

Text language has become an acceptable means of talking among your friends, but remember that applying for jobs requires a more formal response and it is not acceptable for textspeak to transfer into this arena.

Voicemail message

When applying for roles, remove any joke voicemails and record a standard message asking the caller to leave their name and contact number. The use of music, jokes or funny phrases should be avoided.

Answering your phone

When answering your phone, be professional as you never know what opportunity lies on the other end of the line. A badly answered call indicates to a potential employer that you lack customer service skills. Is this how you will answer the phone to their clients?

Qualifications

List your qualifications in chronological order, stating the institution from which you gained the qualification, the date and the grade. Qualifications should be listed with the most recent first. Ensure accuracy in this section as employers will want to see certificates supporting your qualifications.

brilliant tip

How to prepare for pre-employment screening

Companies use pre-employment screening to verify the information provided by a candidate when applying for or being offered a job. This ensures there has been complete honesty and full disclosure from the candidates at an early stage of the recruitment process, which substantially reduces the risk of a company investing time and financial resources in an inappropriate hire.

When applying for graduate roles, candidates should:

- provide correct identification details which can be supported with a valid passport or driving licence
- ensure all qualifications can be verified by the institution from which they were attained
- declare any criminal offences, where relevant to the role
- ensure all previous employment information and references are accurate and true.

There is a wide range of checks available, from previous employment reference, credit and criminal record checks, right the way through to international referencing, educational qualification checks, directorship searches and identity verification. These checks can be applied on a selected basis, depending on the requirements of the hiring company, type of position the candidate is applying for and the level of risk that the candidate will have in their new role.

With more and more businesses realising the importance of background screening and crucially the potential impact of not screening a new candidate effectively, it is almost certain that candidates will experience some form of pre-employment screening.

Rupert Emson, Vero Screening

Writing a profile

The profile is a summary of your brilliance. You will need to highlight your achievements, strengths and key skills. Remember to review the skills required for the role you are applying for and ensure you make reference to these skills here. An employer should read this statement and think WOW! This is where I would encourage you to blow your own trumpet.

Here is a profile checklist:

- The profile should be no more than six to eight lines.
- The first sentence should be a strapline which summarises your key skills and achievements.
- Use action verbs which suggest efficiency and effectiveness, such as managed, delivered, achieved, etc.
- Avoid overused common terms such as communication and teamwork and instead highlight specific tasks. For instance, 'I delivered a winning presentation', which inherently highlights strong communication skills.

● Include details of your skills and knowhow relevant to the
position with reference to your work experience.

brilliant tip

Five top tips to make your CV stand out

Lose the anonymity and include a photo of yourself: Adding a
photo to your CV is not mandatory but it does put a face to a list
of skills and experience. It allows you to stand out from the pile of
similar CVs that consist of only text. And believe it or not: recruiters
are also people and people just like (seeing) people.

Add a personal statement: Starting off your CV with a personal
statement about your strengths and goals gives it a definite boost.
Similarly on Magnet.me, a strong headline will help you stand out
from the rest of the generic headlines ('Looking for a challenge'
probably being the most common). It is one of the first things a
recruiter looks at and allows them to quickly identify you as a strong
candidate.

Use approved templates and forget the glitter: Rather than
struggling to get the layout right, just use a standard template to
create your CV. It is not only much easier but also looks professional
and allows you to do it quickly. You can always customise the
colours and fonts to your liking but don't go mad. Lots of colours,
headers, borders and images is definitely going to make your CV
stand out – but not in a positive way.

Keep it relevant: We are sorry to break it to you, but the babysitting
job you took on when you were 16 is not going to help you get a job
as a graduate trainee at a multinational or a lawyer at a prestigious
law firm (or marketing internship at a start-up for that matter). Make
sure you only include relevant things in your CV. Put the important
things at the top and leave irrelevant experiences out. If you don't, it
only shows you are not able to make choices.

Describe what you accomplished, not how you accomplished
it: Most CVs demonstrate a function and then go on to explain
the responsibilities. However, it is obvious that as a social media
manager you regularly updated the company's Facebook and
Twitter. A recruiter is much more interested in your accomplishments
and impacts such as 'I grew the Facebook community by 40%, grew
our user base by 20% thanks to a Facebook campaign I set up'.

Vincent Karremans, Founder and Managing Director, Magnet.me

Work experience

As an undergraduate your work experience may be limited,
but list all of your previous employment, starting with the most
recent. For each post state the following:

- job title
- date of employment (including start and end dates)
- brief description of the role, highlighting key
  achievements such as employee of the month awards,
  cost-saving recommendations, commitment, customer
  service skills, etc.

If, on the other hand, your work experience is quite extensive,
include the last ten years with a summary of anything of signifi-
cance before. If there are any gaps in your dates, provide a note
explaining the reason: July 2007 to September 2008 Gap year –
travelling around the world.

Voluntary and extracurricular activities

Often if students lack work experience, they can demonstrate
their employability skills through their extracurricular activities. Highlight the skills relevant to the role to emphasise your
suitability.

Hobbies and interests

Include a few lines about your hobbies and interests as they can make an interesting talking point.

✗ brilliant dos and don'ts

What to do and not do when writing your CV

✔ Be meticulous – spelling mistakes, inconsistency in dates and general errors instantly land your CV in the reject pile.

✔ Spend the time making your CV as marketable as possible – writing a CV is not a quick task.

✗ Don't use the same CV for several jobs. Employers want to see how you will fit a specific role, so amend your CV to the skills required for each application.

✗ Don't use cheap paper – the quality and cleanliness of the paper reflect you as a person.

Covering letters

A covering letter is a brief letter that:

● tells the reader why you are writing to them

● states why they should read your CV or application

● thanks them for their time.

It should have three main paragraphs which highlight the role you are applying for, why you are interested in the role and how your strengths demonstrate the competencies outlined in the job description. The standard of your covering letter sets the tone of your application. Incorrect spellings, how it is addressed and the wording all make statements about your attention to detail and the level of effort applied to constructing the letter.

All too often companies receive letters addressed to the wrong person with silly spelling mistakes and not specifically tailored to the role being applied for. Remember that this is your marketing document and the presentation and content will be the deciding factors on whether or not a company will take your application further.

brilliant tip

How to write a covering letter

- Use plain white photocopy paper (expensive paper is not essential as the selling point will be the format and the content).

- The length should be about one page of A4.

- Address the letter correctly. If the name is stated, use 'Dear Miss Smith', ending the letter with 'Yours sincerely'. If the name is unstated, use 'Dear Sir or Madam' ending the letter with 'Yours faithfully'. Where possible, find out who the letter should be addressed to as it makes it easier if you wish to follow up.

- Quote the reference for the job (if there is one).

The first paragraph should provide a strong introduction and reason for your letter. Make reference to the role you are applying for and where you found the advert. Highlight why you are interested in the role and also the company.

Review the job description and demonstrate how your skills relate to the competencies listed in the job description. Be very clear and concise on how your skills match those required. Summarise your overall strengths and why you would be an asset to the company.

In the final paragraph, state any particular dates that you will be unavailable for interview. Then thank the employer for the time spent reading your covering letter.

Yours sincerely/yours faithfully depending on who the letter is addressed to, followed by your signature and your name printed in full underneath.

Common errors with covering letters

Here are some common errors:

- Not customised to reflect the skills and competencies highlighted in the job description.
- Addressed to the wrong person.
- Silly spelling mistakes that spell checking and proofreading would have spotted.
- Not stressing the reasons for the candidate being the best person for the job.
- Too long – covering letters should be clear and concise.
- A scattergun approach, sending letters with no specific relation to role or company.

Application forms

Your application determines whether you will be successful in being selected for an interview. The form represents your first formal communication with the company, so it is important to give a good first impression. When completing online or written applications, be clear when the form needs to be submitted by as applications received after the deadline won't be considered.

Read through the job selection criteria and the job description and map these against your skills and experience. This will enable you to clearly demonstrate your suitability. Use a wide variety of examples, both academic and non-academic. Read and answer all of the questions as an incomplete form will be rejected.

Competency-based applications will ask you to provide examples to outline when you have demonstrated the specific competency. The application will require specific examples, where you will be asked to provide details of your experience and the impact or results of your actions.

Here are some competencies that you may be required to demonstrate on your application:

- adaptability
- teamwork
- effective communication
- self-motivation and drive to succeed
- client focus
- leadership.

If you are completing a handwritten application, photocopy it first. Do several drafts before attempting to complete the actual form. Remember there is no excuse for mistakes and mis-spelt words. With online applications, you are usually able to save the form or your progress to date. Ensure that you draft your answer and read it through before submitting.

You may feel that you need to book a skills session on CVs and applications with your careers service.

Answering competence-based questions

Employers often look for candidates who can display evidence of their capabilities against key competencies as part of the application process. The competencies are based around the skills they feel are important for success in their company. This might include team-working skills, problem-solving, a particular technical ability or softer skills like communication or planning and organisation.

Most employers are very open about the competencies they look for and the first step to completing a strong application is to research them. Application forms regularly include competency-based questions so you'll need to think about situations where you have demonstrated your skills in these areas. These examples, which might come from experiences you have had at university or elsewhere, will form the basis of your application.

Employers love to hear about examples. Your past performance is often a good guide to your future potential, but don't just limit your examples to situations where everything went wonderfully well. Talking about an experience where things did not go quite to plan can be valuable, especially if you can show that you have learned lessons that you can apply in the future to do a better job.

The CARL acronym is a great way to structure these examples: outline the **Context** of the situation you faced, talk about the **Actions** you took, describe what happened as a **Result** and then summarise what you **Learned** from the experience.

brilliant tip

Top tips for application forms

- Tailoring your approach will make your application distinctive. Why do you identify with this organisation over and above their competitors? What is it about this role that excites you? Which of your strengths do you think will be the most useful if you get the job? The more personal your application, the more it stands out from the crowd.

- Use examples that you can expand on if you are invited to interview, and remember to talk about what 'I did' rather than what 'We did' to make it clear what *your* role was.

- Writing a good application takes time, so don't leave it to the last minute. Employers don't always stick to deadlines and may close a vacancy early if they feel they have enough good candidates.

- Care and attention to detail is very important. Read the questions carefully, stick to word limits, use clear, concise language and check your spelling and grammar. A sloppy application suggests that you'll adopt a similar approach in the workplace.

- Keep a record of all your applications. If you are called for interview at a later date you need to know what you have already told that employer, and this can be hard to remember if you have made applications to lots of companies.

Gary Argent, Graduate Transitions

What to wear for a pre-interview

To dress up or dress down? Many organisations have adopted a dress-down policy in relation to staff who are not customer-facing. As a result, on a day-to-day basis staff can be seen to be wearing very casual wear to work. Always remember they are on the inside of the organisation and already work there. You, on the other hand, are trying to get on the other side of the wall. As a result, it is always best to create a good first impression by adopting a more traditional sense of dress for an interview. This way the company knows that if you are required to present to a client you can dress appropriately.

---

brilliant example

Putting your best foot forward

It's amazing how just wearing a suit can boost your confidence. I always wondered how I would fit into this corporate world, as my background is very different from this world. Today on interview day I knew everything I had learnt and experienced throughout my degree would stand me in good stead. When I walked into that interview room I knew I was truly putting my best foot forward.

What do we mean by a 'traditional sense of dress'? A navy blue or black suit. This is applicable to both males and females. Women should avoid tops that reveal too much cleavage, heels over two inches and tight-fitting clothing. A court shoe with up to a two-inch heel would be more suitable.

Avoid making any fashion statements, so piercings, radical hair-styles and tattoos should be avoided at all costs. These may be appropriate while at university, but do not transfer well into the world of work. If you have dyed your hair a bright colour while studying, dye it back before applying for jobs. Once you get the job you can be as radical as you like, when you have proven your worth, but until then stay within the guidelines.

Males	Females
Navy blue or black suit	Navy blue or black suit (knee-length skirt)
White shirt (ironed)	White blouse (ironed)
Plain tie	Simple jewellery and make-up
Polished black shoes	Polished court shoes (up to a two-inch heel)
Black briefcase	Black briefcase

If you are confident in the way you are dressed this will translate into your overall appearance of being a confident candidate. Dress to impress as first impressions are formed within the first 30 seconds.

brilliant dos and don'ts

What to do and not do before an interview

✔ Do your research before attending the interview.

✔ Do not be afraid of LinkedIn stalking the people interviewing you. Research them and their background before. Find out what you have in common with them. Perhaps they have an article online which says they support a certain football team or their LinkedIn page shows they attended the same university as you. Draw reference to it.

✔ Introduce yourself to reception or security. The interview begins as soon as you step foot onto their premises.

✔ Prepare yourself for difficult interview questions such as what was the last mistake you made at work or university and what you learnt from it. Also questions around your development areas and weaknesses.

✗ Don't come to an interview after you've been shopping, even if you arrive to the area to early. Do not see that as an opportunity to do some clothes shopping and bring the bags to office. Even leaving these with reception while you attend your interview is not professional.

X Don't wear too much make-up or fragrance. This can be distracting and off-putting

X Don't forget what you've written on your CV – even what you've listed as your hobbies. Be prepared to be asked what the last book you read was if you've listed reading as a hobby.

Krystle Siaw, HR Manager, Premier Foods

Planning your journey

Arriving late speaks volumes to interviewers. In just ten minutes you have demonstrated:

- an inability to project-manage your journey
- a lack of organisational skills
- a lack of time management
- lack of respect for their time.

As you can imagine, unless there has been a natural disaster there is no excuse for being late. Ways to avoid being late include the following:

- Do a practice run of the journey, so on the day you know exactly where you are going and how to get there.
- Plan your journey so you arrive at least 30 minutes early and allow time for train delays or cancellations.
- If the journey involves you travelling long distances, see if you can stay with a friend or relative who lives closer.

Researching the company

Knowing about the company and the industry is an important part of interview preparation. This demonstrates to the interviewer that you not only want the job but also want to work for their company. Having an understanding of the industry, their competitors and the challenges the company faces shows initiative on your part and will make your answers more relevant.

There are many sources to access information about companies:

- company website
- annual report
- industry magazines
- Google alerts for current information.

tip

How to create a Google Alert

1   Go to www.google.co.uk/alerts

2   Create an alert. Type in the company name.

3   Options – choose the frequency of the updates.

4   Type in your email to create the alert.

5   Add additional alerts such as the industry sector and competitors.

6   Google alerts will help you to increase your commercial awareness and ensure you are knowledgeable about the challenges and opportunities in your sector

The handshake

A crushing handshake can leave the interviewer dreading shaking your hand on exit, but a weak, wet handshake is not impressive either. So practise shaking hands so you have a firm handshake that exudes confidence.

brilliant tip

Five top tips for a Brilliant handshake

1 Make eye contact and smile.

2 Extend your hand.

3 Take a firm grip.

4 Shake the hand up and down two or three times.

5 Say your name.

Getting this right takes practice, so use your careers service, your friends or lecturers to not only practise but also receive feedback on your handshake. It is important that you get this right as this brief exchange makes a statement about your confidence and self-esteem.

Preparing a presentation

Communication skills are an essential part of any role and students may be asked to prepare a three, five or ten-minute presentation as part of the interview process. As with any presentation, it is essential that you understand the task. Presentation topics can range from current topical discussions in the media, understanding the current challenges facing the industry or demonstrating why the company should hire you.

The main challenge of the presentation is to capture the essence of your key points and convey these points within the time specified.

Here are some examples of presentation questions:

● What are the challenges facing the industry?

● Do you think a university degree is value for money?

● Why did you choose to apply to our graduate scheme and how will you add value to the organisation?

- Should senior executives still receive their bonuses even though their organisation has made a loss?

- How do you think technology will change our industry and the way we work in the next ten years?

What makes a successful presentation? Although every presentation is different, there are key ingredients for success:

- Understand what the question is asking you.

- Research the topic.

- Identify two or three key points.

- Develop a clear structure: Introduction, key points and conclusion.

- Time management is essential.

- Practise, practise and practise.

---

brilliant example

Making a presentation

I was excited to read the letter confirming that I had been invited to the assessment centre, but less thrilled that as part of it I would need to prepare a five-minute presentation on the following:

- Why they should offer me a graduate position.

- What I would bring to the organisation.

- What were my expectations of the organisation.

Although the presentation was only five minutes, the research and preparation took one whole week. I had really underestimated how long it would take to not only research the presentation, but also to make sure I had captured everything within five minutes. This was a real challenge, but it all paid off in the end as the panel were impressed and offered me a graduate position.

An engineering graduate

When reviewing your presentation the panel is judging your ability to communicate and organise your thoughts. Your preparation and research will be evident, as to deliver a short presentation you will need to have completed considerable preparation beforehand.

Your verbal communications skills are paramount, but also your body language throughout the presentation. In those five minutes an employer will be able to assess your dedication to the task and how well you prepared, which is an indication of how you will work in their organisation.

Do not dismiss the five-minute presentation as a simple exercise. It is actually a chance for you to shine and show your ability to interpret instructions and deliver to a presentation to a high standard.

Preparing questions

Don't forget that the interview is your chance to find out more about the organisation, so come prepared with a few questions about it. Your research of the company may have raised some questions, but try to avoid questions about salary. Although this may be at the forefront of your mind, with your increasing student loans, avoid focusing purely on the financial aspect of the role. (The job advert should have given some indication of salary bracket.)

Questions can focus on the following areas:

- What are the next steps following this interview?
- What is the career development and progression for someone at this level in your organisation?
- Use your research to formulate a question in relation to the company's current climate.

brilliant tip

How to prepare for an interview

● Prepare, research and understand the company you are applying to – they will want to understand your motivation for applying.

Think about the activities, work placements or projects that you have been involved in and consider how you could use them to demonstrate key business competencies such as leadership, influencing, teamwork, etc. Organisations will all use slightly different words but the key competencies they are looking for will be similar.

● Don't over-rehearse because you may be thrown by different interview styles or techniques.

Helen Alkin, Head of Future Talent Recruitment,
Marks and Spencer plc

brilliant tip

What to do and not do at the interview

● Remember that the interview is a two-way interview. Be prepared to ask your interviewer questions.

● Be confident even if you're not usually. Fake it but don't be arrogant.

● Smile. It's important to smile and be at ease. It will automatically put the person who is interviewing you at ease too.

● Don't be defensive or aggressive.

● Don't fidget as it can be very distracting.

● Don't forget to sell yourself. Too many candidates answer questions with 'We did'. You are not in a group interview, so show what you did and why you are the right person for the role you are interviewing for.

Krystle Siaw, HR Manager, Premier Foods

Interview skills

The interview is your chance to demonstrate why you are more suitable for this job than any other candidate. Central to a successful interview is preparation, but how do you prepare for the unknown? This section aims to provide information about the format of the interview, the structure and possible questions. More importantly, the tools for you to communicate your excellence without saying a word.

Types of interview

Interviews vary depending upon the size of the company and the sector. Often the invitation to the interview will provide more information. Below are the different types that are commonly used.

A panel interview

A panel interview is not as bad as it sounds. Representatives for the panel will be drawn from interested parties such as human resources, the manager and the technical specialist (if applicable). The panel will sit in a row on one side of the table with you on the other (the same format as a firing squad!). Prior to attending you will be given the names of the panellists. Shake hands with each member of the panel and, when answering their questions, try to make eye contact.

A series of interviews

Most interviews will adopt the format of a first and second interview followed by an assessment centre or series of tests. The interviews are usually conducted by the line manager, followed by a senior manager accompanied by a representative from human resources. In some cases, the interview with human resources is conducted separately. The benefit of having one-to-one interviews is that you can build a rapport on an individual basis.

A telephone interview

Telephone interviews are becoming more frequent. Candidates are given a time to expect a call from the interviewer when the details of the name and person will also be provided. Be ready. Don't be caught on the hop. Find a quiet place to take the call.

Because the interviewer cannot see you, your diction, intonation and pace become even more important when delivering your answers. You could sit at a desk to sound professional on the telephone. It is very easy for the interviewer to tell if you are still lying in bed.

Make sure you are well prepared as how you perform will determine if you are selected for the next round of interviews.

brilliant tip

Top five tips for a telephone interview

- Find a quiet place to conduct the interview.
- Ensure there are no technical issues with your phone.
- Review the job description and your application form.
- Research the company and the challenges faced by the industry.
- Practise responding to interview questions.

A video interview

Skype and video interviews are becoming more commonplace. This also creates another dynamic as the interviewer can now see and read your body language. The preparation for the interview is the same, but avoid any technical issues as this will knock your confidence. So check all the equipment prior to the interview.

brilliant action

Practise a Skype interview

Skype interviews are often used as a screening tool, because they allow an employer to interview you without the need for travel, and at a time that suits you both.

Preparing for a Skype interview involves many of the same steps as a normal interview, but because you won't meet your interviewer the experience will feel different. Some Skype interviews will be 'voice only' without a video connection, and the lack of non-verbal communication offers an additional challenge, because you can't see the person you are talking to, and they can't see you.

It is important to practise before you do the real thing. Set up a mock Skype interview with a friends or a careers advisor to get used to conveying your message without the normal non-verbal cues. If your Skype interview is going to include a video link use your computer's built-in video camera to practise, recording yourself answering questions and watching yourself to see how you come across from the interviewer's perspective.

A Skype interview might seem daunting at first, but you can turn the situation to your advantage. Have your application form or CV to hand to boost your confidence. You could write down bullet points for examples you wish to share, sticking post-it notes around your screen so they are easy to see, and jot down a couple of questions that you want to ask at the end of the interview.

The more prepared you are, the more confident you will feel.

Gary Argent, Graduate Transitions

brilliant tip

How to prepare for a Skype interview

● Make sure you have somewhere quiet to do the interview, where you are comfortable and will not be disturbed, and with a stable internet connection which won't drop out.

● Think about the lighting and background and what the interviewer will see behind you.

● Be prepared. Have a drink of water ready to combat a dry throat, and a pen and paper to take notes.

● Dress as you would for a normal interview. Wearing a suit or smart business attire will put you in a professional frame of mind. This is especially important if there is going to be a video link.

● Remember to smile when you are talking and if the recruiter is not using a video link, consider standing up. Both of these techniques will help you to project your voice and make you sound more confident.

Gary Argent, Graduate Transitions

Interview structure

Whether you find yourself in a panel interview or a one-to-one interview, the structure will be similar. The interviewers will try to relax you with a general question, possibly about your journey or the weather. Do not ramble on and on about this (unless you are going for an interview with London Transport!). Recognise that this is just a warm-up question, so keep it brief.

The interviewer will then ask you a series of questions that draw on the selection criteria and the skills required for the post. Tailor your responses and examples to the question being asked. Take some seconds to ensure you understand the question and have a good example to support your answer.

brilliant tip

Take your interview letter

When attending an interview I always bring along the interview letter, just in case I forget the contact name due to nerves. The letter also reminds me of any specific details of where to go on arrival.

A business graduate

Interview questions

What will they ask you? The job selection criteria and the job description will provide you with the hints and tips you need to prepare for possible interview questions. A good framework to use is STAR: Situation, Task, Action, Result. This framework encourages you to provide specific examples to demonstrate both the competencies and the behavioural criteria outlined in the selection criteria. Read both the job description and selection criteria and identify key skills (usually marked as E for essential).

Situation – Think of a situation when you have demonstrated the skill. Try to use examples that are drawn from your course, but also from extracurricular activities.

Task – What was your aim or purpose?

Action – What was your role? Outline your actions.

Result – What was the outcome?

To practise, give examples of when you have demonstrated the skills listed below.

	Situation	Task	Action	Result
Leadership				
Team-working				
Organisation				
Project management				
Initiative				
Commitment				
Determination				

Here are some other possible questions:

- Why do you want to work for . . . ?
- What do you think you can offer . . . ?
- What are your strengths and weaknesses?

brilliant dos and don'ts

What to do and not do at the interview

✔ Listen to the questions or brief you are being given so you don't go off track.

✔ Dress appropriately, in line with the role that you have applied for.

✔ Give yourself time to read, understand and plan for the exercise and think about the points you want to make – for assessment centres specifically.

✘ Don't worry if you need to take a few seconds to formulate your answer in your head before responding.

✘ Don't panic at an assessment centre, even if you feel one exercise has gone badly. The decision will be based on your performance and each competency will be rated more than once, so all is not lost.

Helen Alkin, Recruitment Manager,
Marks and Spencer plc

Non-verbal communication

During the interview it's not always what you say that makes a difference, it can be what you do! Your appearance will make an impact and other factors are your posture, facial expression and how you walk. These actions all talk to the employer about your suitability, so make sure they are sending the right message. If you are prone to slouching when you walk or sit, correct this for the interview. A confident walk sends the right message when you enter the room.

Eye contact is essential. Try to build some rapport with the interviewer by looking at them when you speak. If you are addressing a panel interview, make eye contact with the person who is asking the question, but during your response try to look at the other members of the panel as well. This is easier said than done: it takes practice. Make use of your careers service to practise your interview techniques.

brilliant tip

Stay focused throughout

Your exit is just as important as your entrance. I was so excited that the interview had gone well. I was able to answer all the questions. My preparation had paid off. We shook hands and I turned to exit. Forgetting that we were in a glass office, I walked straight into the glass door. I tried to recover quickly, but you could see the amazement on their faces. I composed myself and exited successfully on my second attempt. My advice is stay focused till the end of the interview and your exit needs to be clean. By the way, I did get the job.

An IT graduate

Psychometric tests

Psychometric tests are often included in the selection process and can take various forms. The most common tests are:

- verbal reasoning
- numerical reasoning
- personality.

Companies will often inform you which of the above will be involved in the test.

How do you prepare? Prior to attending you can take practice tests. Your careers service should have a selection of practice tests, but you can also go online to www.shl.com, where you'll find the majority of tests used by employers. You can then practise the sample tests online.

> ⟨**brilliant** tip⟩
>
> How to prepare for psychometric tests
>
> - If appropriate, get in touch with the prospective employer and ask for more information about the tests. For example, what does it measure? How long does it take? Are tools such as a calculator allowed for a numerical reasoning test?
>
> - Do some research. Look for more information via the test publisher's website and explore whether you can sit online practice tests to familiarise yourself with the type and format of questions that you are going to face. If you are unable to find examples of the exact test, practising other tests measuring the same ability will help. However, if this is the case, be prepared for a different look and feel when you sit the real thing.
>
> - Ability tests will have a set time - normally around 20 to 40 minutes. Rehearse concentrating for that length of time, either

via practice tests or an activity related to what you will be measured against.

- If you are sitting a verbal reasoning test, practise reading such material as editorial from a reputable news source or industry-related information. Similarly, apply the same preparation to abstract or numerical reasoning assessments.

- Personality assessments are designed to discover whether you are a potential fit to the organisation. Any inconsistencies in your answers are likely to be picked up by the employer, so it is best to be true to yourself. It is of no benefit to either party for you to work somewhere where your values conflict with the organisational culture.

- Prior to the test exercise, sleep and eat well. The key to performing well in any test is to be calm yet alert. Feeling good when you begin the test will significantly improve your chances of giving a true representation of your ability. Naturally, the opposite also applies.

- Sit the test with no distractions. This ideally means in a room by yourself, with phones and anything else put aside that could steer you off course.

Matt Stevens, Pearson Talentlens

Assessment centres

Companies often save the best till last, so the assessment centres are often the final hurdle in the interview process. Due to the expense of running an assessment centre, only the candidates who have true potential are invited.

What can you expect? They allow companies to observe you in a range of settings to see how you cope. As a result, the assessment centre is made up of a series of individual and group tasks.

An observer will be assigned to each candidate and make notes and grade you in relation to the selection criteria. Often you are not required to prepare any material, as the observer wishes to observe how you approach the given tasks and your interactions with the rest of the group. There are no right or wrong answers to many of the exercises, but they are interested in your methods of deduction and handling of data.

Exercises enable the company to observe a number of skills that you will have discussed in previous interviews. The assessment centre allows observers to see at first hand how you meet the selection criteria. Skills tested can include:

- communication
- team-working
- decision-making
- initiative
- leadership.

Here are some tips for tasks you might be set.

Task	Description	Tips
Mini case study	The mini case study will provide the information for a given task. Candidates will be required to use the information to formulate a response.	Don't panic! Build your response. Identify factors that will affect the decision, highlight additional information needed and state the reasoning for your response.
Presentation or report	The presentation or report is often linked to the mini case study and candidates are asked to present their results either verbally or in a report.	Present a structured response. Practise your presentation skills beforehand. The careers service will have skills sessions available.

(continued)

Task	Description	Tips
In-tray exercise	This exercise is as it sounds. Candidates are given an in-tray consisting of emails, letters, messages and so on, and the task involves prioritising and preparing responses to the requests.	There is no right or wrong answer so be clear in the reasoning behind your decisions.
Interview	As above.	
Group discussion	The group will be given a mini case study or task and has to prepare a response collectively.	Listen to points made by other candidates. Make clear and constructive contributions to the discussion. Read between the lines to find out what is implied but not stated.

brilliant example

The value of assessment centres

Assessment centres offer the opportunity to put candidates into contextually appropriate and role-relevant scenarios. They provide us with an opportunity to see candidates performing across a breadth of different activities that enables assessors to be confident in the hiring decisions that they are making.

The fact that every candidate will be seen by every assessor also means that the decisions are based on a robust wash-up and discussion process across assessors rather than being down to one individual.

From a student's perspective it also means that the decisions are not based on the performance of one exercise alone.

Helen Alkin, Head of Future Talent Recruitment, Marks and Spencer plc

Post-interview

The interview is over and there is nothing you can do to change your performance. But it is good to reflect upon what went well and what you would change for next time. Learn from every interview as the more you do the more experienced and ready you will be for the next one.

Reflect on the examples you used to answer the questions. Were they sufficient? Were you clear in explaining your role and the actions you took? Don't be impatient and call the company the next day for the result. Wait to be contacted.

brilliant tip

Top tips for interviews

● Ask for feedback if you have been unsuccessful so that you can learn for next time.

● Follow up with the organisation if you have not heard anything in the time they had specified.

● Don't give up if you are not successful first time – there is more than one way to access opportunities in an organisation.

Helen Alkin, Head of Future Talent Recruitment,
Marks and Spencer plc

● Shake the interviewer's hand and thank them for their time.

● Remember that the interview hasn't finished until you've left their premises.

● Don't inundate them with calls and emails for feedback. If they say you will hear back within a week, only chase after the week has gone, but in a respectable manner.

Krystle Siaw, HR Manager, Premier Foods

brilliant recap

- Use your careers service.

- Identify how your existing skills translate into skills valued by employers.

- Identify any skills gaps and create an action plan to develop these skills.

- Preparation is central to all elements of the selection process.

- Research the company, the industry and its competitors.

- Think of relevant examples to selection criteria drawn from both academic and non-academic activities.

- Use STAR to structure your answers.

- Remember that communication is both verbal and non-verbal.

- Always remember that you only get one chance to create a first impression, so make it a good one.

CHAPTER 10

Your employability journey

We are currently preparing students for jobs that don't yet exist . . . using technologies that haven't been invented . . . in order to solve problems we don't even know are problems yet. (Fisch and McLeod, 2013)

To ensure a Brilliant future you really need to understand what employability means to potential employers, your degree discipline and more importantly to you. The landscape within which we work is continually changing. The demand for a skilled workforce is paramount for the success of the company and also to the growth of the economy.

Despite the fact that both employers and universities make provision for the development of employability skills through the availability of work experience, ultimately the key driver of your development of employability skills is you. You will determine your level of engagement and to what degree you get involved.

That is why it is important to fully understand the 'I' in the I Brand employability model, as despite all the opportunities available, students' experiences will vary in relation to their levels of effort and involvement. This further emphasises the importance of your 'individual brand' as everyone will be different: students differ in the priority they give to developing employability skills and their interpretation of what employability means to them.

Why is employability important?

Changes in the higher education sector will continually increase the importance of employability not only for students, but will also place the onus on universities to ensure they are producing graduates who can 'hit the ground running'. The increase in fees has put employability at the heart of higher education, as students leave with unprecedented levels of debt.

Success will be defined in terms of their ability to secure employment, especially with the expectation that they will become liable to repay tuition fees once their salaries surpass £21,000. Currently students are able to see the employment statistics for each course and so make informed decisions about where to study and which course to do.

Employers place a heavy emphasis on employability skills, as although they recognise their role in the development of graduates, they also see the importance of graduates harnessing and developing their own skills. This is increasingly more important with 72% of students graduating with a 2:1 or a first (HESA, 2015). That is why extracurricular activities, especially those which demonstrate your ability to function outside your comfort zone, become increasingly valued with employers. This shows drive and ingenuity, which will always be valued in any sector.

Students who are able to practically demonstrate and draw on examples that show their understanding of generic employability skills will advance far quicker in the graduate market. Do remember that employability does not guarantee employment, but definitely enhances the prospects of graduates to secure employment.

The statistics highlighted in 'The Graduate Market 2016' (High Fliers Research, 2016) emphasised that a third of all graduate vacancies in 2016 will go to graduates who have previously worked at the organisation and students with no work experience will struggle to secure a graduate role.

Employability will continue to increase in importance, and universities, employers and students need to place more emphasis on developing ways to attain these skills while the students are at university. Universities actively promote activities and employers have increased their provision of opportunities to engage with their organisation through more open days, insight days, work experience and placements.

What is employability?

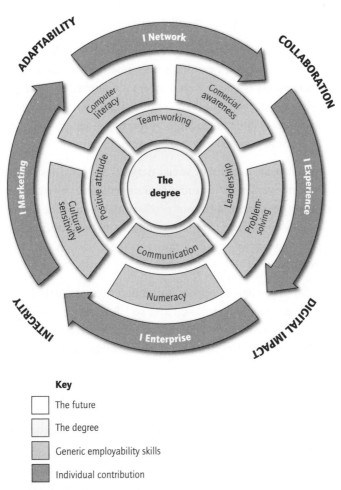

Key

- The future
- The degree
- Generic employability skills
- Individual contribution

I Brand employability model

Graduate employers recognise a range of generic employability skills that underpin the ability of a graduate to perform in the workplace. The I Brand employability model recognises there are skills embedded within your course, but there is a need to develop practical examples of generic employability skills drawn from extracurricular activities, work experience or voluntary work.

The 'I' in the model recognises your individual effort and contribution. The model acknowledges that your background and personality will influence how you engage with employability both within a course and extracurricular activities.

Networking is key in gaining employment and identifying opportunities. Your extended network is dependent upon your background and ability to widen your network via parents' associations and business contacts. This can create a significant disparity in opportunities available to students, as it is dependent not on ability but the social and economic standing of parents.

The increased availability of social networking provides access to a wider network and so students are not limited to who they know. It allows students to join professional forums and meet professionals in the field. Students will need to be confident and willing to step outside their comfort to meet and engage with professionals.

Your ability to recognise opportunities and take calculated risks is part of your personal make-up and so I Enterprise recognises a students' ability to add value through innovative and creative approaches to tasks. Enterprising skills are highly valued among employers.

I Marketing draws heavily on the analogy of marketing a product and encourages students to review all aspects of their marketing strategy. How will they promote their product in the marketplace? How will they stand out? This is an important aspect of the model as students need to understand their strengths and weaknesses – essentially, their unique selling point – in order to communicate this factor to potential employers. Every student should be able to answer the question: 'Why would an employer choose me over another graduate?'

The I Experience highlights and emphasises the different backgrounds, cultural differences and motivational drivers for each student. Student experience is unique and personal to each student so it is important to recognise this factor when developing employability skills. Students bring their 'personal baggage' to the table and ultimately it will impact their engagement and development of employability skills.

The outer layer

The outer layer of the model: Collaboration, Digital impact, Adaptability and Integrity are all elements to help you future-proof your employability. These are the skills and traits needed to operate within the twenty-first century workplace.

Collaboration will become increasingly import with organisations seeking to work globally, drawing on a multitude of skills, from a multitude of workers, located in a multitude of countries.

Adaptability is key to your future employability as change is inevitable and so you need to demonstrate flexibility and creativity to ensure your skills are aligned with the changing landscape.

Integrity is a must with the ethics of organisations being brought into the public domain.

Finally, digital impact focuses on how technology is disrupting your industry and the skills you need to develop to survive. Overall, the circular nature of the model highlights the ongoing process of developing your employability skills.

Whose responsibility is it?

Ultimately, the responsibility rests with the student. Universities clearly have a role to play in providing opportunities to develop employability skills in the curriculum and through the provision of extracurricular activities. Employers have a responsibility to ensure the provision of varied work experience opportunities. In the end it all comes back to the students' willingness to partake in these opportunities. Each student's level of engagement will vary.

What opportunities exist?

Employability is embedded in the curriculum. Through various methods of assessment, students are given the opportunity to develop a range of skills. The key issue is that these opportunities are seldom labelled as such and so few students actually connect the dots and recognise the transferable nature of the skills they develop on their courses and their relevance to the world of work.

Vital skills are learnt and honed during assessment, which will not only develop essential skills for the workplace but also for the interview process to secure a graduate role. The table below (repeated from Chapter 1) reinforces the connection between assessment methods and the skills required in the workplace.

Assessment method	Transferable skills
Group assignments	Students are often required to work in teams to complete a group task. Students develop project management, team-building, negotiation and influencing skills, all highly relevant to the world of work.
Presentations	The ability to develop a well-structured presentation that communicates the key points effectively and efficiently is a valuable skill, useful in a variety of situations beyond a degree.
Case-study analysis	Case-study analysis presents a business scenario and requires students to utilise critical thinking, analytical and problem-solving skills not only to identify the key challenges, but also to make recommendations drawing on both the internal and external environments faced by the organisation. Case studies are often used within the selection process to differentiate candidates.
Report writing	Accuracy and clarity in report writing is a must. Literacy skills are central to academic studies and for application forms and writing reports or emails in the workplace.
Problem-based learning	The ability to resolve problems and provide well-founded solutions is directly transferable to the workplace, where students will be continually presented with challenges.

Assessment method	Transferable skills
Research	Research skills are applicable to all industries. The ability to collate, synthesise, analyse and clearly present information found can add value to all organisations, whether private, public or third-sector. All industries are reliant upon information to provide insights into current industry dynamics, future trends and possible opportunities and threats in the marketplace.
Personal development planning	PDP encourages reflection on strengths and weaknesses and develops self-awareness, which supports continual development and learning.
Examinations	Examinations present the opportunity to apply an understanding to scenarios or questions within a time constraint. Many professions use professional examinations to test candidates' knowledge and application of the subject matter. An ability to pass examinations is a required skill within the workplace.

The other avenue for developing employability skills is through extracurricular activities. Both on and off campus, students have the opportunity to develop skills through involvement with the student's union or undertaking internships or voluntary work. It is through this practical application and demonstration of employability skills that students enhance their ability to stand out, especially when they can no longer rely on the degree as a unique selling point.

These activities not only enrich the student experience but also provide a wealth of examples to draw on in an interview or selection process. Once again, it relies on the students' ability to both recognise and connect the skills they are developing to the generic employability skills valued by graduate recruiters. Below is a recap of some of the skills that can be developed through extracurricular activities and how they relate to the world of work.

- **Leadership skills:** You don't have to be the president of a society to develop leadership skills. Taking ownership of a task or role and demonstrating the ability to influence, negotiate for resources and motivate others to achieve a common goal are all examples of leadership qualities. These skills will resonate with an employer, as one of an organisation's goals is to identify people who have the ability to lead or manage a team.

- **Project management:** Whether you are at university or in the workplace, you will always need to have a clear plan of action of how you will achieve your goals. The ability to plan, adhere to deadlines and identify key milestones to succeed are all part of the organisational skills required within the work environment.

- **Event management:** The coordination and planning involved in organising a successful event demonstrate strong organisational skills and the ability to multi-task. Event management requires a high level of organisational skills, from liaising with speakers and developing and distributing the marketing communication to negotiating additional resources. The ability to coordinate a successful event is an impressive addition to your CV. The busy workplace will always require the ability to multi-task while maintaining standards. Organisational skills and the ability to meet deadlines are musts for successful graduates.

- **Budgeting:** The ability to budget and forecast demonstrates an understanding of how decisions will affect the bottom line. For instance, understanding how to budget for the costs associated with an event and balance these costs in relation to ticket sales to break even and or make a profit are valuable skills. All organisations will value these skills and will especially value your ability to highlight the relationship between decision-making and the impact on costs, as the economy requires all industries to operate efficiently. These skills are directly transferable to all industry sectors.

- **Communication:** Both written and spoken communication skills can be developed by participating in a university society. The ability to write a persuasive email or report requesting support for the society or the development of effective marketing materials, providing members with updates and information, are useful skills. Employers will expect a high standard of literacy and communication skills. You will be required to produce reports, communicate with clients and provide information to other departments in the organisation.

- **Networking:** Networking will help the enterprising student secure additional resources for their society and generally meet individuals from different backgrounds and interests. Networking is the backbone of all business. The ability to maintain a wide network is useful not only for university but also identifying possible opportunities.

Employability is a continual process. This is reinforced by the circular nature of the model. While at university and beyond you will continue to develop your employability skills and also redefine which skills are important to you and prospective employers.

Are there jobs out there and can I have one?

Good question. When all is said and done and students have done all they can to develop employability skills, will they be rewarded with a graduate role? The graduate opportunities in 2016 are on the rise and the outlook is more promising, but students cannot afford to be complacent.

Companies have raised the stakes and many require an upper second as the minimum for entry to their graduate schemes. More than a third of all graduate vacancies go to students who have previously undertaken work experience with the companies concerned. As a result, students need to understand the importance of not only developing employability skills but also establishing links with companies during their studies.

Work experience has become a vital ingredient in a graduate's ability to secure employment. Ninety percent of the top graduate recruiters offer work experience opportunities for graduates in the form of both internships and placements (High Fliers Research, 2016). The competition for these positions is fierce and students have to undergo a series of selection processes in order to be successful.

When I grow up I want to be a . . . ?

Choosing the right career is often one of the most difficult decisions. How do you know you will like your chosen career path? Knowing yourself will be the best starting point. Having a good understanding of what motivates you and what is a priority for you in the workplace will help you not only identify suitable roles but also suitable companies.

This can be supported by undertaking research into possible career options, both discipline-related and unrelated. There are many successful professionals who have not taken the automatic career path for their degree discipline.

Learning from the experiences of alumni is also another option. Alumni can provide insight into career options and their own experience of the working world. Regardless of your discipline, there will be various roles available to you and it is always useful to speak with professionals in these roles to find out whether the role is suitable for you.

Internships and placements also give you a different perspective about a role. There is no substitute for work experience to provide a behind-the-scenes look at possible career options. The opportunities also allow students to experience the culture of the organisation and decide if it is a good fit.

This can be easier said than done. Finding work experience and ultimately a graduate position is not an easy feat. An internship provides you with the opportunity to see if a career is for you, and also provides an employer with the opportunity to test-drive your product. If you are not fortunate enough to find an internship, there are other ways to gain work experience. Temporary roles or job shadowing are also methods of gaining a practical insight into a potential career choices.

Communicating your employability

The ability to translate your employability skills into those valued by employers is an art in itself. Identifying your strengths and weaknesses and areas for development is essential when trying to find both work experience and graduate roles. The ability to communicate your Brilliance will rely heavily on your verbal and literacy skills and your ability to present yourself both physically and on paper in a manner acceptable to employers.

Preparation is central to all of the elements of the selection process, from writing your CV to attending your first interview. Your success will be underpinned by planning, researching the company and the role, reflecting upon your experiences and identifying how they match the selection criteria.

Using the STAR framework – Situation, Task, Action, Result – to review your work experience, tasks undertaken on your course and extracurricular activities will help you to match your skill set to the requirements of your employers. You will be surprised at how many examples you will be able to draw upon.

Being meticulous in your preparation at all the stages of the selection process is paramount. An error on your CV or arriving late for an interview speaks volumes about your character and creates a bad impression. If you cannot manage yourself, how will you manage any of the business relationships or processes?

Researching the company and having knowledge of their main competitors, the challenges they face in the marketplace and a general understanding of the business environment will support you in your interview and add value to your responses. Employers will be impressed if you take the time to find out not only about their company but also any challenges faced by the organisation.

Prepare, prepare, prepare, as it can make the difference between a successful application and being overlooked in favour of another candidate.

A continuous career life cycle

Employability is not an end in itself. Once you begin your career, you need to continually reflect upon your employability skills to check they are still aligned with the needs of your employer and the industry sector. Students need to reflect on how their industry or organisation and more importantly their role will be affected by the continual changing landscape within which businesses operate today.

IT is continually changing and influencing sector development. Social media has had an impact on all sectors in some way, with companies using social networks both informally and formally. You can't afford to stand still when you secure a graduate position, as life is constantly moving.

---

brilliant example

Don't get in a rut

After you've been in the workforce for a few years, or even a few months, it's easy to get stuck in a rut or a routine. Expanding your skills on a regular basis is a great way to avoid burnout, encourage growth and prove to colleagues and employers that you are willing to stay active, hungry and curious in your career.

General Assembly offers classes, courses and workshops – online or at our campuses around the world – to help adults learn the latest skills in today's most in-demand topics across design, marketing, technology and data. We teach the critical skills and tools you need to either level up in your career or change paths altogether. For instance, update traditional marketing skills with our part-time Digital Marketing course or take your data analysis to the next level with our Data Science courses.

Or are you ready to learn full-stack web development? Our full-time, immersive Web Development course not only prepares you to become a junior web developer but incorporates career coaching and job placement support as part of our education-to-employment approach.

Professionals can always rely on General Assembly to teach the most in-demand and relevant skills and by making learning a priority, you will open new doors that you never knew existed.

Julien Deslangles-Blanch, Regional Director,
General Assembly London

The continuous process of employability

As you develop, mature and move through your career life cycle, your needs and wants will also change. What you defined as career goals and ambitions may change as you get older or your circumstances change.

The circular nature of the I Brand employability model emphasises the continuous process of employability. You will continue to grow and develop and this in turn will inform your employability. Your degree is a three- or four-year course and throughout that time you will be exposed to many different experiences that will influence the direction of your future career.

University is a time to explore, research and investigate various career options and the skills required. There are also many opportunities to build and develop your network, both within and external to your university, so don't miss out.

▶ brilliant examples

Postgraduate study

The key benefit of a postgraduate or professional qualification is the steer it can give towards a real specialism, which can ultimately act as the gateway to a specific career or potentially higher earnings. Research shows that individuals with a postgraduate qualification earn more over their career than those without (Department for Innovation and Skills, 2016).

If you want to work in many professions, such as accountancy or law, a professional qualification is a necessity. Postgraduate qualifications are also increasingly aligned with professional ones. This has to be a good thing for students and employers alike as it may help to save on future training costs and time.

Like an undergraduate degree, the relevance of a postgraduate qualification may not always be immediately apparent when you embark on the first steps of a professional career. Often its benefits emerge gradually as you progress into more senior roles, where the deeper skill sets and knowledge that you developed are required.

Will Holt, Dean/Director of Pearson Business School,
Pearson College London

Professional exams and postgraduate study

Professional exams provide an opportunity for you to become a specialist within your field of study. Your knowledge and skills are updated with the current thinking in the industry and you will have the opportunity to become a specialist in your field. These skills will add value to your employer and also avoid your skills becoming outdated.

brilliant tip

Why take professional exams?

- Professional qualifications are practitioner-based and will add a layer of practical knowledge that a degree may not be able to provide.

- Many employers will insist that job applicants have a professional qualification or are prepared to study to gain one.

- Similarly, many employers require existing employees to gain a professional qualification as part of their personal and career development.

- Many employers are willing to pay the cost of tuition, assessment fees and professional body membership.

- There is always more to learn. Studying for a professional qualification will help you keep up to date with the latest developments, trends, innovations and techniques in your chosen field.

Philip Preston FCIM, Network Manager,
The Chartered Institute of Marketing

Professional qualifications enhance your career

While qualifications require investment in time and finance, they have a positive impact on your employability by providing a rigorous external assessment that demonstrates your competence, knowledge and skills.

They are invaluable at key points in your career to do the following:

- Gain essential underpinning knowledge when entering a new role.

- Show existing experience already gained on the job.
- Create a springboard of knowledge and skills to facilitate a promotion.

brilliant action

Gain a professional qualification

The value of a professional qualification goes far beyond the knowledge, skills and certificate gained. It links you to a network of professionals studying on the programme who will provide wider insights to develop your perspectives.

Undertaking accredited courses during your career demonstrates a commitment to professional development to stay up to date in our fast-changing world.

In addition, most industries have a professional institute which people with an appropriate background can join. Qualifications are a means to gaining membership of such bodies which can provide you with additional professional recognition, excellent development resources, advice and networking opportunities.

Research shows that qualifications boost earning potential over your working lifetime.

Andy Lancaster, Head of Learning and Development, CIPD

Get involved with corporate social responsibility

Corporate social responsibility (CSR) is a great way to give back to society by volunteering in initiatives supported by your organisation. It can also develop your management skills. It provides a wealth of opportunities to enhance your experience within the working world and helps you stand out when seeking your next promotion.

▶ brilliant examples

Get on a CSR programme

The perpetual evolution of technology has put the world at our fingertips. We now have instant access to news and information from around the globe. But as boundaries become less defined, the need for continual education and improved understanding of different cultures and societal issues has become more acute.

Many companies now have formal CSR programmes which integrate their business into the wider community, helping to address the concerns of stakeholders and providing a platform for community-related collaborations. Employees have a key role to play in supporting CSR strategies – by volunteering their time, skills and expertise they can bring about meaningful and positive change.

While volunteering is a valuable community resource, it also delivers benefits by providing unique opportunities for skills development and character building. The activities through which these personal development and educational openings are available are diverse in themselves, for example, mentoring a student, reading to a child, sitting on the board of a charity or helping a community organisation to craft a marketing plan. Each present their own challenges depending on your life experiences but are equally beneficial in their own right.

Businesses are constantly adapting to their changing environment and look for employees who are adaptable and well-rounded, who seek out ways to understand the broader context of the business environment and the ways different organisations and cultures operate.

Volunteering is an excellent vehicle for achieving this and demonstrating a plethora of positive traits – ambition, thoughtfulness, creativity – to current and future employers.

Patsy Francis, Director of Community Affairs, UBS

The need to be determined in your search for a career is paramount. Building your employability skills while at university is not an option but a necessity. You cannot afford to ignore your employability until after graduation. Start building and developing your employability skills from day one to get ahead of the game.

It does not stop there. When you find your first graduate position, you need to continually update your skills to not only keep your position, but to advance. When seeking a promotion, you will need to demonstrate how you add value to the organisation. This can be demonstrated with the addition of new skills and knowledge.

In today's workplace and the continual development of new skills and technology, employees must update their skills to maintain their competitive advantage.

brilliant recap

- Make sure you understand what employability means for your discipline and potential graduate recruiters.

- Determine to what degree you engage with developing employability skills.

- The success of a university is strongly linked to the ability of its graduates to secure graduate employment.

- The responsibility of developing employability skills rests with the students as they have to make an active decision to engage.

- Students need to recognise the opportunities embedded within their courses to develop transferable skills relevant to the workplace.

- Extracurricular activities provide students with the opportunity to give practical demonstrations of their employability skills in action.

- Leadership, project management, event management, budgeting and communication are all skills that can be developed through extracurricular activities.

- Undertaking professional qualifications further develops your employability skills

- Continually updating your skills is a must.

- Employability is a continual process and each stage of your career will require you to redefine the skills you need to develop in order to progress.

- Take every possible opportunity to network and develop links with companies while studying.

- Take time to explore both discipline-related and non-discipline-related career options.

- Gain work experience in your chosen field as this is a good test to see if this career is for you.

- Be meticulous in your preparation at all stages in the application process.

- Employability is not an optional extra – place it at the heart of your university experience.

What did you think of this book?

We're really keen to hear from you about this book, so that we can make our publishing even better.

Please log on to the following website and leave us your feedback.

It will only take a few minutes and your thoughts are invaluable to us.

www.pearsoned.co.uk/bookfeedback

Useful resources

Further reading

Bothwell, E., (2015) Top 25 UK Universities for Graduate Employment, Times Higher Education https://www.timeshighereducation.com/features/top-25-uk-universities-graduate-employment (accessed October 2016)

Browne, Lord John, (2010) 'Securing a sustainable future for higher education: An independent review of higher education funding & student finance', government paper www.independent.gov.uk/browne-report (accessed June 2011)

Bright, J. et al. (2013) Brilliant Graduate CV: How to Get Your First CV to the Top of the Pile, Harlow, Essex, Pearson Education

Hodgson, S. (2014) Brilliant Answers to Tough Interview Questions, Harlow, Essex, Pearson Education

Done, J., et al. (2016) Brilliant Graduate Career Handbook, Harlow Essex, Pearson Education

Jay, R. (2014) Brilliant How to Succeed in any Interview, Harlow Essex, Pearson Education

Jones, D., (2004) Foreword, Prospects Directory, Prospects

Maher, A. and Graves, S., (2008) Graduate Employability: Can higher education deliver? Threshold Press

McIvor, B. (2008) Career Detection: Finding and Managing your Career. Management Briefs

Mortimer, N., (2015) *'Lloyds Bank digital transformation chief – 'we are in danger of just becoming the plumbing'',* The Drum, 17 June 2015 http://www.thedrum.com/news/2015/06/17/lloyds-bank-digital-transformation-chief-we-are-danger-just-becoming-plumbing The Drum 2015. (accessed October 2016)

Norton, T., and Thomas, H. (2009) 'Beyond the curriculum: Opportunities to enhance employability and future life choices'. Policy report of the 1994 Group's Student Experience Policy Group www.1994group.ac.uk/documents/public/Publications/BeyondTheCurriculum_Nov09.pdf (accessed June 2011)

Ries, E. (2010) The Lean Startup: How Constant Innovation Creates Radically Successful Businesses, New York, Portfolio Penguin

Yorke, M., (2006) Embedding Employability into the Curriculum. Higher Education Academy, Enhancing Student Employability Co-ordination Team

Useful websites

Association of Graduate Recruiters: www.agr.org.uk

British Universities & Colleges Sport: www.bucs.org.uk

Do-it.org www:do-it.org.uk

The Duke of Edinburgh's Award: www.dofe.org

Graduate Talent Pool: http://graduatetalentpool.direct.gov.uk

Frances Trought: www.francestrought.com

High Fliers Research Ltd: www.highfliers.co.uk

Higher Education Careers Services Unit: www.hecsu.ac.uk

Inspiring Interns www:inspiringinterns.com

National Council for Graduate Entrepreneurship: www.ncge.org.uk

Prospects: www.prospects.ac.uk

Rare Recruitment: www.rarerecruitment.co.uk

SHL: www.shl.com/TryATest

Target Jobs: www.targetjobs.co.uk

Young Enterprise Scheme: www.young-enterprise.org.uk

References

AGCAS (2011), Employability: An AGCAS position statement http://agcas.org.uk/assets/download?file=2262&parent=725 (accessed June 2011)

Association of Graduate Recruiters (2016), Annual Survey 2015: Graduate Recruitment 2015

Bransford, J. and Stein, B. (1984), The IDEAL Problem Solver, New York: WH Freeman

CBI (2009), Future fit: Preparing graduates for the world of Work www.cbi.org.uk/pdf/20090326-CBI-FutureFit-Preparing-graduates-for-the-world-of-work.pdf (accessed June 2016)

CBI/EDI (2010), Ready to grow: Business priorities for education and skills: Education and Skills Survey 2010 www.cbi.org.uk/pdf/20100501-cbi-education-and-skills-survey-2010.pdf (accessed June 2016)

CBI (2011), Working Towards Your Future http://www.nus.org.uk/Global/CBI_NUS_Employability%20report_May%202011.pdf (accessed October 2016)

CBI (2015), Education and Skills Survey 2015: Inspiring Growth http://www.cbi.org.uk/news/cbi- pearson-education-and-skills-survey-2015/

CMI (2014), 21st Century Leaders: Building Practice into the Curriculum to Boost Employability http://www.managers.org.uk/~/media/Files/PDF/21st_Century_Leaders_June2014.ashx (accessed September 2016)

Cutlip, S. and Center, A. (1952), Effective Public Relations, New York, Prentice Hall

Dearing, Sir Ron (1997), 'The reports of the National Committee of Inquiry into Higher Education' (Dearing Report) www .leeds.ac.uk/educol/ncihe/nr_007.htm (accessed June 2011)

Department for Business Innovation and Skills (2016), The Graduate Labour Market Statistics: 201 https://www.gov .uk/government/uploads/system/uploads/attachment_data/ file/518654/bis-16-232-graduate-labour-market-statistics-2015.pdf

Development of Economics Ltd (2015), The Value of Soft Skills to the UK Economy: A Report Prepared on behalf of McDonalds UK http://www.backingsoftskills.co.uk/The%20 Value%20of%20Soft%20Skills%20to%20the%20UK%20 Economy.pdf (accessed October 2016)

Diamond, A., et al. (2008), Global Graduates: Global Graduates into Global Leaders file:///C:/Users/Mauby/AppData/Local/ Temp/CIHE%20-%201111GlobalGradsFull.pdf (accessed October 2016)

European Commission (2016), The Erasmus Impact Study, Regional Analysis

Fisch, K. and McLeod, S. (2013), Preparing Students for What We Can't Prepare Them For, Teaching and Learning in Higher Education https://teachingandlearninginhighered .org/2013/07/15/preparing-students-for-what-we-cant-prepare-them-for/ (accessed October 2016)

Friedman, T. (2005), The World is Flat: A Brief History of the 21st Century, New York, Farrar Straus Giroux

Goleman, D. (2014), Working with Emotional Intelligence, New York, St Martins Press

Govindarajan, V. and Gupta A. (1998), Success is All in the Mindset, Financial Times

Higher Education International Unit (2016), Gone International: The Value of Mobility http://www.go.international.ac.uk/sites/default/files/GoneInternational2016_the%20value%20%of20mobility.pdf (accessed 10 December 2016)

Higher Education Statistical Agency (2014/2015), Outward Mobility Data http://go.international.ac.uk/sites/default/files/HESA%202014%20to%202015%20printable%20analysis_2.pdf (accessed October 2016)

HESA (2015), Destination of Leavers in Higher Education https://www.hesa.ac.uk/news/30-06-2016/sfr237-destinations-of-leavers (accessed October 2016)

High Fliers Research (2016), The graduate market in 2016 file:///C:/Users/Mauby/AppData/Local/Microsoft/Windows/INetCache/IE/885FYRZU/GMReport16[1].pdf (accessed October 2016)

Institute of International Education, The Role of Study Abroad in Global Education file:///C:/Users/Mauby/AppData/Local/Temp/GSA-Teacher-Resource-1-An-Overview-of-Global-Education-and-the-Role-of-Study.pdf (accessed October 2016)

Karinthy, F. (1929), 'Chains' in Everything is Different (out of print)

Kotler, P., Armstrong, G., Wong, V. and Saunders, J. (2016), Principles of Marketing (electronic resource) 16th Edition, Harlow, Essex, Pearson Education

Mayer, J. D. and Salovey, P. (1997), What is emotional intelligence? In Salovey, P. and Sluyter, D. J., (Eds.), Emotional development and emotional intelligence: Educational implications (pp. 3–34), Harper Collins, New York

McNair, S. (2003), Employability in Higher Education, LTSN Generic Centre/University of Surrey

OECD (2013), 'How many students study abroad and where do they go?' in Education at a Glance 2013: Highlights,

OECD Publishing, Paris http://dx.doi.org/10.1787/eag_highlights-2013-12-en

Peters, T. (2004), In Search of Excellence: Lessons from America's Best Run Companies, London, Profile Books

Reimers, F. (2011), Introduction : Why Global Education? What is Global Competency? Harvard www.sd25.org/superintendent/GlobalEducation.pdf

René, C., The Students' Guide to Networking (unpublished work)

Robbins, L. (1963), Higher education report to the committee appointed by the Prime Minister under the chairmanship of Lord Robbins, 1961–63, HMSO. Chapter 2, para 25, p. 6

UK HE International Unit (2016), Gone International: the value of mobility, report on the 2013/14 graduating cohort

UNESCO, Institute for Statistics (July 2014), Top 20 Destinations for International Students https://www.theguardian.com/higher-education-network/blog/2014/jul/17/top-20-countries-international-students (accessed October 2016)

Willets, D. (2010), House of Commons debate, 8 July 2010, Column 511, Daily Hansard – Debate www.publications.parliament.uk/pa/cm201011/cmhansrd/cm100708/debtext/100708-0001.htm (accessed June 2011)

Yorke, M. (2006), Learning and Skills Series One: Employability: What it is and what it is not. Higher Education Academy, Enhancing Student Employability Co-ordination Team

Zhang, L., The Interview Technique You Should Be Using https://www.themuse.com/advice/the-interview-technique-you-should-be-using#! (accessed October 2016)

APPENDIX

I Brand
worksheets

What is employability?

Below is a list of employability skills valued by employers. At the beginning of the academic year rate yourself on how well you have developed these skills. Rate yourself out of 5, with 1 being 'very well' and 5 representing 'needs development'.

	1	2	3	4	5
Computer literacy					
Cultural sensitivity					
Commercial awareness					
Team-working					
Problem-solving					
Numeracy					
Positive attitude					
Communication					
Leadership					

Review your degree programme and highlight any degree-specific employability skills.

1	2	3	4	5

If you have scored 3 or below, develop an action plan to further develop these skills (see the next worksheet).

Action plan

Skill	Importance	Action	How you will demonstrate	Date for completion
Example: team-work	In the workplace you will be required to work in teams	Join student society or sports team	Take on a specific function in order to draw on examples of specific actions taken	End of academic year

Your degree

Employability is embedded in your degree programme. Make a list below of the units for each term and identify the employability skills you are developing. Review the assessment methods, current industry/sector information, guest speakers, etc.

Subject	Employability skills

Review the feedback on your assignments and reflect upon your self-management when completing the tasks. What did you do well and what areas need further development? Consider, for example, how you managed your time, interacted with others, how well you researched the topic, etc.

Now use the table below to identify the top three areas to focus on in the following term.

Area for development	How you will develop this skill and by when

Use the STAR matrix to develop these examples into possible answers for application forms.

Situation: outline the situation

Task: define the task

Action: action you took

Result: the outcome?

Skill	Situation	Task	Action	Result
Leadership				
Teamwork				
Communication				
Positive attitude				
Problem-solving				

The continuous use of this framework will enable you not only to review your development of employability skills but also your ability to relate examples drawn from your degree to skills valued by employers.

Freshers' fair checklist

A freshers' fair is usually held at the start of the academic year to provide new students with the opportunity to find out about the students' union, clubs and societies and other extracurricular activities.

Who is the president of the students' union? Make a note of name and contact details

Make a list of all the societies at the university that are of interest

Make a note of their contact details and the date of the next meeting

What other extracurricular activities are available at the university?

Make a list of other activities you might want to join and note their contact details

If you are interested in starting your own society, email the president of the students' union to find out how

Is there a society related to your specific discipline? If yes, join. If not, this is a perfect opportunity to start a new society.

Voluntary work and you

Assess your availability and identify possible volunteering opportunities. Create a timetable that highlights your lecture and study times, your part-time job, society meeting times and the days and time you would be willing to volunteer. Remember you can volunteer in your holidays and so it does not need to conflict with your schedule at university.

Monday	Tuesday	Wednesday	Thursday	Friday	Saturday	Sunday
9.00						
10.00						
11.00						
12.00						
13.00						
14.00						
15.00						
16.00						
17.00						
18.00						
19.00						

Websites to search for volunteering opportunities:

www.do-it.org

www.timeoutdoors.com

www.volunteering.org.uk

Your university careers service

The graduate market and your industry/sector

1   Ask your course director or careers service for the statistics on destinations of leavers from your course.

- Which employers have recruited from your course in previous years?

- For what roles are students from your course typically recruited?

- Did students in previous years undertake internships and placements? If so where and for whom?

2   Review 'The Graduate Market in 2016' by High Fliers Research. What are the graduate recruitment statistics for your sector?

3   Ask your course director if it would be possible to speak with the alumni of your course to gain from their experiences following graduation.

4   Identify sector-specific magazines or journals to keep you abreast of changes in the sector.

5   Find the professional body that represents your sector. Note its name, contact details, student subscription fee and any networking events. Then sign up for its e-bulletin.

Start your own business

1   What business support is offered at your university?
    - Name
    - Contact details
    - Enterprise training
    - Grants and funding

2   Is there a student enterprise society?
    - Name
    - Contact details
    - Meeting times

3   Does your university operate a small business incubator unit?
    What support does the unit offer to current students?
    - Contact name
    - Contact details
    - Location

4   Is the university involved in any enterprise competitions?
    - Name
    - Details of the competition
    - Entry requirements
    - Closing date

Part-time job review

Whether you are stacking shelves or frying burgers, you are developing your employability skills. This exercise will help you to translate your part-time skills development into skills valued by a graduate employer.

Job title:

Outline the key functions of your role:

How does your function contribute to the overall success of the company?

If your role disappeared tomorrow, what impact would this have on customer experience?

How do you think your skills could be considered in a wider context in relation to:

● customer service

● leadership

● project management

● organisational skills

● team-working

● problem-solving

● communication

Use the STAR matrix to review and demonstrate some of the skills outlined above.

Skill	Situation	Task	Action	Result
Leadership				
Teamwork				
Communication				
Positive attitude				
Problem-solving				

Getting to know you

Conduct a personal review of yourself and distribute it to at least five others who know you in differing capacities: lecturer, colleague, fellow student, etc. Your personal review will provide an insight into your strengths and areas for development.

1 = very good to 5 = needs development

Traits and skills valued by employers	1	2	3	4	5
Punctual					
Reliable					
Attention to detail					
Problem-solving					
Communication (oral and written)					
Numerate					
Innovative					
Positive attitude					
Honest					
Meet deadlines					
Accurate					
Can think on your feet					
Organised					
Team player					
Leader					
Negotiator					
Influencer					
Name one strength					
Name one area for development					

Employability workshops available on campus

You should attend free workshops at your university, often run by the careers service. Throughout your degree and as you progress in the development of your employability skills, you will need to revisit previously attended workshops and your needs and wants will change.

The process of applying for an internship, placement or graduate role are very competitive and these workshops can help you review what you have to offer a potential employer.

Workshop	Date booked	Location
Application forms		
Developing a CV		
Covering letters		
Interview skills		
Assessment centres		
Psychometric testing		
Job-hunting skills		
Communication skills		
Assertiveness in the workplace		
Leadership skills		

Your individual brand

What does your brand say about you? Write a short statement (no more than 100 words) that captures your unique selling point: what makes you stand out?

This statement should capture the skills developed on your degree and through your extracurricular activities. You should also capture your 'I', your individual contribution to tasks – what you bring to the table as a team member, leader and project manager.

Continually revisit this statement, incorporating your new skills. Compare your statement from year one to your statement in your final year.

Personal statement: year one
Personal statement: year two
Personal statement: year three

Index